Strange Times

Strange Times

Tales From American Strippers

Elle Stanger

Copyright © 2015 Elle Stanger
All rights reserved.

ISBN: 150032390X
ISBN 13: 9781500323905

*"Everything in the world is about sex,
except sex.
Sex is about power." – Oscar Wilde*

Contents

Prologue · ix
Mine · 1
New Girl · 9
Live! Nude! Girls! · 18
Three Little Words · 25
Silver Lining · 33
Marilyn · 38
How I Met Svetlana · 50
Cheeques · 61
From Elation to Emptiness · 67
Haikus, An Intermission · 73
A Sixty-Something Persian Guy Peed On Me and All I Got Was $20 · · · · 75
Jersey Girl · 80
Darlin' · 84
Occupational Hazards · 91
Audition Story · 97
The Regular · 103
Strip Story · 111
Doggy Style · 134

Prologue

Viva Las Vegas

WELCOME, LADIES AND gentlemen, to Strange Times. The title is apt: for some reason, when getting naked for money, in spite of its legality and its at-times utter prosaicness, shit gets strange. Sex work is, after all, generally frowned upon by society. It takes a certain kind of girl to buck convention and dance around buck naked. Mostly, I'd say, it takes a tougher, more enlightened type, cuz to put up with societal disdain on a daily basis can certainly be a drag. But the proof remains in the pudding: our work—stripping—nurtures, heals, and inspires—on both sides of the stage.

It's really not all that shocking, sex work. It's monotonous and thrilling, inspiring and depressing, prosaic and sublime. What IS shocking is how society likes to judge it. This still amazes me, eighteen years into my career as an all-nude girl. Even people who make a habit of examining issues from every angle like to get lazy and stereotype sex workers. This judgement isn't merely ignorant, it's harmful. I hope that every soul that cracks this compendium of strippers' stories finds its mind cracked open, as well. After all, such books didn't always exist. Huge swaths of forest have fallen over the centuries to accommodate the exploration of sexuality by men.

But when women do so, they are frequently gagged, sometimes metaphorically, all-too-often literally. I consider it a huge step forward that sex workers' stories are being voiced, published, and read.

A stripper's life is so filled with stories, it's not surprising so many of us are writers as well. Our stories run the gamut of experience and emotion; it's not all sunshine and rainbows, or Tequila Sunrises and raining money. But the common thread I've long noticed—in dressing rooms as in this book—is the love—love for our clientele, our work, each other, and ourselves.

From Elle's incredibly evocative dressing room lecture to a newbie, to the sting of judgment and subsequent healing in Katie B.'s prose poem, as when Brody explains that her motivation to dance is inspired by giving pleasure to others, the theme, as I see it, is love. There's more love in Sophie's story of the affection between a working girl and her customer, and in Clementine's tale of transformation—a painful, powerful journey of one woman's discovery, through stripping, "... what it meant to be a woman, to claim space, the necessity of self-worth in the midst of a hundred hungry eyes." Are these stories salacious? Some of them. Scandalous? Hardly. These are the tales of working women, teasing out themes common in the dark corners of table dance areas, the covens that are dressing rooms, and the bright red-lit stages across the country.

Love can bloom in the darkest of places. The alchemy of the stage—the glitter, the music, the costumes, the lights—can create the most amazing transformations, for performers and audience alike. But mostly, it's the love. Love that, like the tales in this book and that fifties song that so many of us have peeled off our panties to, is strange.

Mine

Lux ATL
Atlanta, Georgia

Prelude

Granny Sue was a beautiful woman, Momma told me. I am a beautiful woman, Momma told me. You will be a beautiful woman, too. She brushed my hair hard. Take off your shirt, she said.

Soon you will start your period. Eventually you may grow some breasts. Here's hoping, she sighed, as she busted a pimple on my shoulder. Hand me that cream.

You'll need make-up, Momma told me. This skin.

I am going out tonight. Your father may come home. If so, please tell him Mother is out.

Purity is irreplaceable, Momma told me as she lit a cigarette. You come from a line of Southern belles. Aunt Erma was Miss Pittsylvania County, remember that. No one forgives a bad woman. The men, they can do what they want. But the badness of women, it can't be undone. Not in this world.

A black ash dropped from her cigarette into the toilet with a thud.

She painted her lips red with a brush.

Put your shirt back on, she ordered.

Eyebrows must be plucked, Momma told me. Blackheads extracted. Nails shall remain painted—nails tell a lot about a girl. She pushed the tiny pointed buds of my breast together and laughed. Well, keep your accent, Momma told me, the fellas like a drawl.

She leaned deep into the mirror above the sink and curled her eyelashes one last time. She kissed the mirror, leaving her lips' print smeared on the glass. She smoothed the blonde curls round her face with a nod. This here is more valuable than mansions and fancy cars, she said.

Leave this on for thirty minutes, Momma told me, and handed me a fat tube smeared with green clay. Then remove the mask with a vicious scrub. Next dig the sharpened stick into your cheek and destroy all blemishes. Apply three drops of astringent to a grey stone, mix in one eye of newt and a hair of the dog; chant in Latin—any word will do. Try Pater. Pater. Pater. Pater. I am a beautiful woman. You will be beautiful too.

Mother is going out tonight, Momma told me. If Father comes home, please tell him Mother is out.

How To Do This

Set a goal.

Walk in the club thinking, "I've got to make four hundred dollars tonight." At ten dollars a lap dance, that's forty lap dances.

I used to go home with headaches from smiling all night.

Walk around. Catch an eye. Sit down.

Ask, "How do you feel about corny jokes?" Everyone likes corny jokes.

Ask, "What did the egg say to the boiling water?" Pause. "It said, 'It might take me a while to get hard, I just got laid.'"

Introduce yourself. Make small talk for one cigarette.

Don't smoke? Take up smoking.

If he seems like a country boy, let your accent run wild. If he is in a suit and has a master's degree, tell him you're paying off student loans. If he is Mexican, sit on his lap and speak Spanish. If he's elderly, touch his thigh, smile sweetly, and practice kindness.

Stereotype, for sure. In a room full of strangers it can help.

Do this, over and again, from 8 p.m. until 3 a.m. Expect to make most of your money after midnight.

Some customers are bored suburbanites who want a sex-crazed girl-gone-wild. Some are socially inept and want a friend. Some are ugly and have never been laid. Some are powerful and say "just call me Bitch." Some men are addicted to strippers and you better latch on to one of them real fast because they'll spend some goddamn money. Some of these men adore you and they want you to meet their mother. Occasionally a man will become obsessed with you, and for a while you cultivate the obsession because he's spending a grand a night on you; he's told you his broken life and you never even told him your real name; he was in a war and now he's crazy and you deal with the influx of flowers and stuffed animals at the reception desk, but when you get scared, tell the bouncers you're scared and he won't be allowed in anymore and he won't even know why.

You'll wonder what this does to his real dream-world life.

Don't care.

Case Studies

Test administrator: Tests may involve toothpick geometry, cryptograms, Sphynx-like riddles. He has an MBA to substantiate his paternalistic authoritarian tone. After determining you to be of moderate intelligence, in the tone of a high school principal presiding over a bad kid at a conduct conference he tells you: you could do something better with your life.

Power-reverser: An enigmatic mix of yuppie and darkness in a black suit: the maybe-villain of a David Lynch film. He provides you with a script; instructs you to study the script; returns hours later to enact the script—a script in which you demean him: calling him the "f" word, the "p" word, the "c" word, you defame him. "Why are you here, you fucking f*****, you don't even like p****!" But he does; oh, he does like it.

Middle-aged molester: Wears loose pants—how dare he!—jogging pants, windbreaker pants, cotton pants. Despite the strategic fashions, he spends vast money in the club that his Wal-Mart wardrobe belies. His bald head beading sweat, the lenses on his thick glasses fogged with amused arousal, he whispers innuendoes so dank and perverse that assuredly, you imagine, this man drives a windowless van.

You dunno whash you're mithin: It's late. He's young. He's just enough drunk to want more to drink and recent years of frat house porn addiction drive a frightful hunger: student loans didn't cover his appetite in any way, not tonight, and now he wants to eat for free. Most of his life he's had it all for free. He can only imagine that you're incorrect—that you are wrong, ignorant—that you are too dumb to give yourself to him, for nothing but his gaze in exchange—for nothing. When it costs ten dollars.

I'm Yours

Do you like corny jokes, I ask

I just got back from the golf course, answers the fat old man. He runs his red hand through his wavy white hair and says, Been in here fifteen minutes and I still haven't seen a waitress. Where's the goddamn waitress?

What did the egg say to the boiling water, I ask

The three car salesmen are tan and laughing. In their homes wait babies and former homecoming queens. I don't know, says the leader, what did the boss say to his employees? He says I made three fuckin' sales today, and that's why I'm the boss.

It might take me a while to get hard, I say

Ron lifts his sunglasses and waves me to his table. A bottle of champagne and four girls from the day shift accompany him. It's dark for those shades Ron, but you're not here to look or touch. Ron's boyfriend wrestles with Ron's son on varsity.

I just got laid

Trucker places a cheap cigarette deep within his beard. It's hard to have a lover on the road, he tells me, hard to find love when you're putting it in the wind. Seventy hours a week behind that huge steering wheel and he's round, grizzled, and lonely, but proud of his cooking. I used the crock pot last weekend, he says. I had a girlfriend but she went to jail. But the crockpot roast turned out right good. He strokes his beard and stares at the television from beneath the rim of his baseball cap. I have never seen his eyes.

Trucker buys the usual three minutes of grinding. Reflected by the mirrors lining the walls behind him, my skin glows white under the black light. Leaning over his shoulder, I kiss the cold mouth of my reflection.

I never wanted a whore for a daughter

Look at me, Trucker grunts. The air beats with strobe lights. I search for my eyes in the mirror. I got a nice enough place to live, Trucker says. Whyn't you come to dinner? I'll pay you. I expect I've paid you enough. Maybe I don't pay as much as some of the others. Maybe I ought to send you flowers.

I'm not crazy Momma said don't call me crazy you saw her yourself on her knees

I slide to the floor and lavish my tits upon his thighs. My knees pop when I land and I bury my grimace in his lap. He smells like diesel fuel. Grease stains my fingers.

My own daughter ruined, Momma said and slapped Daddy. Send her away

Trucker holds me hard against him. Look at me, he pleads. He pulls me into his lap.

How dare you suggest—I don't need another rest!

Eyes closed, Trucker pants. I count the final beats of the song and slide from his lap. He sighs and hands me a ten. You ought to come to dinner, he mumbles as he exits the booth. Spent, he exits the club in haste and disappears into the deepening darkness of the parking lot.

If I send her away will you be well again

I lock myself in the bathroom and stand before the mirror, a tube a lipstick drawn like a sword. With my other hand I pull a tit from my sequined top and squeeze it luxuriously. This—this body here, this breast in my hand—this body is mine. This body here, in this mirror, this body is mine. This breast is mine.

I never wanted a whore for a daughter—only fourteen and sucking dick

The lipstick drops from my hand. I push my body back from the mirror and arrange myself for presentation on the stage.

I tell the customers, I tell the Truckers of the world, I'm yours.

Back to Stripping

Sometimes, when I think about going back to stripping, I do feel a little scared. It's been years. I'm older now.

I think, wow, stripping again, and this time I have to show my pussy. I don't want to bend over in men's faces. I wonder, does it have to come to that?

My expenses have doubled since my boyfriend left me, and financially, I never planned on making this move alone. My car is breaking down. But I'm moving to Atlanta, where the clubs are all nude, and I am a stripper. I will also be beginning my Ph.D. in the fall.

I've thought about asking my grandmother for her car: a Buick Le Sabre, silver, huge, automatic transmission, everything I hate. I thought I could say, Hey Granny, why don't you forget about the money you were going to give me for graduation and just give me your car instead? I could tell her, You need a new car, something zippy. But shit. She just gave me a grand a few months ago—the first time as an adult that I've ever taken this kind of money from a family member. Only once have I asked my mother for money—one hundred dollars—which she denied.

I quit stripping for two full years while I've pursued this Master's degree. Grad school has been hard. I'm leaving this town feeling hurt and rejected. I tend to romanticize the stripper lifestyle I once lead. A portrayal:

> Play dress up four nights a week. A constantly shaved snatch. Go out the other three nights a week, buy your friends drinks, get your own for free. Expensive Cuban dinners. Professional manicures. Sleep until one, nap from three until five, shower, work at the club, divide your money into piles of denominations on your boyfriend's bed. Smoke weed. Have a snack. You made eight hundred dollars tonight. Seventeen this week. Go to Vegas. Fuck it.

But in those days, I lived in a house with many friends. I had a boyfriend who adored me. He sent me flowers to the strip club. I wore pasties at work, a thong. I was never really naked. The house was never dark when I came home.

At work men licked me. They put their fingers in me. They came in their pants, leaving my thigh wet. I have always been able to disconnect, and I have studied for history tests mentally while humping a fifty-year-old man's erection.

But I loved going to bars on my nights off, traveling, department store make-up; I loved the constant assurances that I was beautiful. I trekked Japan solo on stripper money. I bought my first car on stripper money. I bought my mother a black diamond on stripper money. Once I drove across the East Coast with $5,000 cash in the trunk just to hit the beaches. Gangster. Outlaw. Glamour. I enjoyed having a bedroom drawer that was consistently filled with thousands of dollars in cash. At times I have placed the money on the bed and rolled around in it. Good God, the new clothes! The new clothes!

Now I'm moving again, and I'm doing it alone. I have no idea what this type of thing entails. My man left me, I'm leaving my friends, and I'm going broke—I'm just fucking going broke. I can barely force myself to go to the grocery store and yet I have to figure out how to move to Atlanta in the midst of all these terrible goodbyes and crushing emotional paralysis. Whenever I think of this situation, all I can think is Yuck. Get this out me. But I've got to be practical.

I have to make money.

I can't ask my grandmother for a car.

I have to pay rent in Atlanta somehow. And get utilities connected. And eat.

The assistantship at the University will kick in eventually, but I'm still faced with two empty months. No income. No friends.

I think: I'll strip when I get there. If I strip, I won't have as much time to be sad. I'll dedicate myself. I'll make a lot of money; I'll buy a new car; I'll write like crazy; I will plan a new show. Maybe I'll play some music. Yet I know if there is a goal I pursue out of these various self-improvements, it will be the money-making. On all the other, more creative pursuits, I can't trust me right now.

But, alone there in Atlanta, coming home night after night to no one and darkness and whimpering dogs, what will I be with only the strip club in my life? Can I be okay with strange men blowing on my pussy if I can't go home and be hugged by a man I love? What if it's four a.m. and too late to call any of my friends, and I've lost the only person I could possibly call in the middle of the night? Can I be okay? Is that a choice I can make?

The new clothes. The new clothes.

There is no limit to what I can afford.

New Girl

Casper Suicide
Portland, Oregon

Okay, so the boss wants me to talk to you. I know you're new because I've never seen you here before and you have that wide-eyed look to you. I've been here about seven years, since the very beginning of this club. And while everyone is always learning, here are some things you definitely need to listen to, and really listen because I may not ever tell you again. This is not inherently an industry of helping. Most clubs you ever step foot in? You'll not be well-received and it's not personal, you're fresh tits. You're competition. And you will receive no help from anyone else. Me? I've dealt with hundreds of new girls and many of them don't last very long. I don't know what you've done in your previous jobs but this may be one of the hardest jobs you ever undertake.

First of all, it doesn't matter if you don't know how to dance right now; you'll figure it out as you go. Watch a couple of basic pole dance videos on YouTube and try to learn something, or at least learn one new trick every time you dance. The day shifts are good for that. Not many people will be in here and it's the best time to learn. Some of the other day-shift girls will probably help you. But, you need to understand that some of us have very unique tricks and we don't like to be copied. Winter will walk from the bar tables to the poker players' table without even knocking over a single candle or losing her footing once. It doesn't matter how drunk she is; it's her trick, she's never failed and no one else attempts it. Gabriella does pull ups from the ceiling to hip-hop music. Sometimes I'll light a match and put it in my pubes and have the birthday boy or girl blow it out. These are all party tricks. But, you can't entertain people with this stuff alone, so I suggest you start figuring out how you are going to move on stage.

I hope you don't get embarrassed easily. Your skin will thicken over time, at least. Get used to the idea that you might start your period on stage, or you may fart during a lap dance. You may have a tampon string hanging out at some point. Topless dancers have it so easy. I've fallen from the pole a couple times, and Mary smacked her head on that big mirror in the corner when she was swinging from the ceiling bars, shattering it immediately. She was fine. Adrenaline helps. Be able to laugh at yourself in front of strangers, or else just cry alone, later.

People are going to want to buy you alcohol, and you don't have to always drink it. Take a sip when you walk away, put it down somewhere and discard it if you want. When I was pregnant I worked for about four months; I wasn't showing. But, I'd take my drink and dump it out and fill it with water in the sink. If it's a choice between making money for my family or giving my unborn a case of fetal alcohol syndrome, what would you do? Anyway, my daughter is two now. She's a genius. Knows all her letters and colors and shapes. What was I saying? Oh yeah, Patrons will buy you more drinks if they see that you're not already holding one. The bartenders and the owners like this because you will rack up their sales, and the customers will like it because you are socializing with them. Oh you don't drink? Okay, good luck with that. I've heard that 1 million times. But, there's nothing like the anxiety of a Friday night with a full house and a shaking set of knees. I'll have a shot at beginning of the evening and sip soda water and vodka throughout the rest if I feel like I need to. You're not any better or worse than anyone if you do drugs or if you don't, or if you drink or if you don't. I don't smoke cigarettes, so I don't bother going out on the patio. That's where most of the dudes will try to get you to sit and talk to them forever, and it's hardly lucrative.

Most of your money will probably come from lap dances, if you are thick-skinned enough to hustle for them. Everybody hustles differently. You'll have to figure out your own way of doing that to. We are not selling our bodies, we are selling our time and our companionship. I gave a soldier a dozen dances before he shipped out to Afghanistan and I gave him two dozen the day he returned, two years later. Men and women come in here for many different reasons, maybe they haven't seen another set of nipples in years, or maybe they just like being surrounded by naked women. There are married, suburban couples who like to feel inspired and mix up their boring, monogamous sex lives. Sometimes escorts will come in with their sugar daddies or clients. You'll be able to spot those, and sometimes the escorts will help you hustle a dance or two. Respect those ladies. They don't have to do shit for you, because they are working too.

However, we are not prostitutes here. The bosses run a pretty clean club, and that means that nobody here is doing extras. All of the clubs in this state and country are different, but here it's a one way fully nude club, period. That means that we get fully nude, serve alcohol and have legally licensed gaming, but that customers do not touch us- for the most part. If you want to have a guy rub your feet or your back that's okay, but make sure his hands don't wander anywhere else. One guy likes to have me shove my underwear in his mouth and I do so, because there's nothing illegal about it. But, don't be fingering yourself or jerk a guy off through his pants. We don't encourage release here. Fuck no. The first time a guy shoots a load in his pants without you even touching him you'll wonder how you're supposed to dance around the jizzy spot on his khakis for the next two minutes. In lots of clubs there are girls sucking dick in the VIP room, but that's not how we make our money. I make plenty of money, and that's because I am a dancer and I am a talker. You'll see.

What else? Get a good suitcase, preferably something that is not porous or expensive because if any other stripper spills her drink in the backstage it might leak onto your stuff. Wash you clothing regularly, and start carrying a sewing kit and some gorilla glue in your suitcase. You'll figure out the other things you need as you go.

As far as the tunes, consider what kind of music you would like to dance to- nothing too incredibly emasculating like Lady Gaga, but believe me that I've heard the same Love and Rockets songs about 500 million times, so feel free to put a unique touch on your stage music. Personally, I dance to a lot of old blues. If you notice the girls have favorite songs that they dance to; don't play those songs. Of course nobody owns the music and we pride ourselves on our own personal tastes here, but everybody knows that when Red House cues up that means that I am on stage. And I like it that way.

There will be guys here that will try to take advantage of you. There will be guys and women here who passively aggressively insult you, and a lot of them won't even realize that they are doing so. You'll learn the best way to answer invasive questions. About the hundredth time that a guy asked me what my boyfriend thought about my job, I figured out to tell them that I don't have a boyfriend because I like being alone. Whether or not that's the case, that usually shuts them up real fast. You'll get hit on a lot, and you might meet a nice boy here but look at these people as if they are wallets, not lovers. I wasted a lot of time and effort hoping that my man friend would pop into the club; it sucked up my focus and it fucked up my game. That's not to say that you won't meet some amazing and truly enlightened people here. One of my favorite clients is a lawyer, another one is an architect and another one is a schoolteacher. I have a handful of married couples that come to visit me, whether or not they live out of state, and sometimes they will get couples dances or dances by each other. You know that means they will probably be having good sex later.

Be polite to everyone but be exceptionally gracious to the best customers. You want to know why I make good money? Because I make people feel special. That's all that stripping really is. The dancing is irrelevant; people come to strip clubs because they want to feel intrigued and they want to feel special. Think about the last guy you dated. I don't even know if you like guys. Whatever. Even if you didn't know what he was doing when he wasn't around you, if he sent you a text message with some hearts you felt special. It didn't matter if you suspected he was sucking other ladies on the side. Maybe he was? The point is that the right strippers and the right lovers will know when to make you feel special, even if you're not.

STRANGE TIMES

Learn to count the money with your eyes. I could pick up and tell you how many there are; it doesn't matter if it's 3476 o 49. Don't let anybody stiff you on stage or in the dance room. A lot of these cheap fuckers have been spoiled by the Internet and they think you are open-legs-on-demand. You can politely remind people that their ass in a seat equals you at least a dollar a song. Fuckers can get up if they don't pay you. We don't dance for free. Well, I don't. You do what you want. Lap dances are different- the bouncers can't help you as much. If you suspect that somebody won't pay you, offer to hold their jacket or have them take their keys out of their pockets. Tell them that you don't want to stab them with their keys or break their cell phone in their pocket. And then if the Dickhead refuses to pay you, grab it, walk to the bouncer and use it as leverage. You will have people run out on you. I've been stiffed probably $100 or $200 in the last few years. Some of them suddenly will become angry when they realized that you aren't going home with them, while others will be too drunk and miscalculated the money that they had in their wallet. Maybe the ATM isn't working that evening. If a guy wants to tip you extra, let him. We are not a commodity, we are a luxury service. If people want to feel fancy and tip the naked lady extra, hell yeah.

Wave to the bouncer or the DJ if someone at your stage isn't tipping you. A lot of people from other states don't know that they are supposed to, so I usually give them a gentle reminder and asked them if they know that it is a dollar minimum to sit at this stage. Some people are really generous but a lot of people are very entitled. I don't know if it's our generation or just the nature of the business. At first you won't really notice, because you'll be too busy trying to figure how to dance without looking like an idiot, but once you have your movements down and your confidence up nothing will become more infuriating than dozens of people leering at you, and especially the rounds of applause you'll receive. Clapping doesn't pay for my mortgage and complements don't keep my belly full, and that is why we hustle for dances.

You'll probably be in the best shape of your life, except for your knees. Your knees are going to be really screwed up for a while, I suggest taking a supplement of Glucosamine, Chondroitin and MSM. I'll write that down. Invest in some Arnica or iron supplements too. You will probably feel like hell and your skin will breakout for the first couple weeks or so, until everything gets used to the physical abuse of the stage. Don't be afraid to smile onstage. Some of these girls would double their money if they could just grin at people. A scared face is not sexy, unless you are a rapist. In that case, I don't want you sitting at my stage anyway.

Get used to the fact that hundreds, if not thousands of strangers will see your naked body, and you will receive nothing for it. Lots of people don't tip. I would say that I make 80% of my money off of 20% of the clientele that set foot in the store. If you're smart you will bring money to pay your stage fee at the beginning of every shift. This way, the pressure is off and you don't have to be afraid that you'll walk home with nothing. A lot of people think that strippers make a shitload of money- and some of us do- but many of us do not, and some girls would do better as janitors, quite honestly. A lot of people think that we make an hourly wage. I'm pretty sure you already know that we don't. The plus side is that you don't have to pay taxes unless the state starts auditing you, but that's pretty rare. Some of the girls regulate themselves and pay taxes as independent contractors. I can point you in a direction. But, let's start you making money first. And no offense, but you might not even be here after tonight.

Don't complain to the bosses if you don't make money; it's not their problem. They have enough to worry about, with advertising costs and liabilities and maintenance and scheduling and food orders. You get the point? I'm not a business owner, because I don't want to have to deal with all that stress, and I don't think they want to deal with my stress either. All of us girls will bitch about the lack of money all night long, and that's because we're usually in the same boat. Misery loves company I guess. That brings me to my next point: don't be surprised if you don't get the good shifts right away. You are new, and you may never get the good shifts, but that's just how it goes. Everybody wants to make the most money, but life is a balance and with the good comes the bad.

This is a job, straightforward. Save your money, track your income. Put 10% to 50% of what you make a week in your savings. If I break my leg tomorrow, me and most other girls don't have any insurance or Workmen's Comp. And how do you explain the gap in your employment for the last few years? I know one girl who fell off her horse and still has metal in her leg; she'll never dance again. I don't know what she's going to do for income, but in this recession? Fuck no, I hope she has a savings.

As long as we're talking about responsibilities, buy some Dial soap and keep it in your shower. You need to shower after every shift. This stage might look all clean and shiny, but I guarantee you it's crawling with E. coli from 100 different people's assholes right now. You know why? Well first of all, lots of people don't wash their hands. Think about all the drunk dudes going in the bathroom, passing out and shooting up and jerking off and maybe even puking, and if any of that mess gets on the floor and they walk out into the main room, well guess what? We are all sharing the same floor on the soles of our shoes and then one of us ladies walk onto the stage we roll around in all of that filth. That's why it's so funny when some pervert tries to lick or kiss me. Doesn't he understand all of the shit that's on my body? Like, literal shit, guy. Just because I look pretty doesn't mean I taste pretty. Some of the girls tease me about being a germaphobe, but I wipe my cell phone down with a Clorox wipe after every shift when I get home, and I don't wear the same clothing after leaving a shift.

Another good reason to use dial: I've had MRSA and staff infections a few times. Lots of girls have. When I went to urgent care the first time, I thought it was an infected spider bite, and maybe it was. The nurse told me a decade or so ago, MRSA only lived in hospitals. Now that shit is everywhere. Some people die from it, mostly babies and elderly people. But still. It's gross and it's painful. See the scar on my ass cheek? I had to have that corked with gauze. Not cute. So yeah, Dial soap.

You'll get used to the hours eventually, I don't know if you have sleeping problems but melatonin helps keep my biorhythms regular on the nights that I'm not here.

Everyone has a shitty night. There will be a couple shifts or weeks that maybe you don't sell many or any dances. And that's pretty bad. It doesn't mean that you're unattractive, but it might mean that you aren't good at conversing with people. A lot of dudes will offer to buy you a drink but won't tip you. See if the bartender will exchange the drinks for money at the end of the night, if she's pouring you fakies. That can get pretty complicated though, and it's actually illegal. So, maybe don't worry about that right now. Don't ever talk about the money that you make. Even if it's not bragging, girls will feel inadequate or competitive. And, it will bite you in the ass. Nobody on shift needs to know if the dude in the dance room tipped you an extra $40 or $400.

It's pretty funny how our society likes to value people based on their career or social standing, but I've learned so much more about the quality of character. I watched a doctor get tossed out a here the other night because he wouldn't quit fondling the dancers. He kept joking about wanting to give us physicals. Some of the best tippers will be the blue-collar dudes: the guys that work in kitchens or in lumber fields. They understand what it's like to literally bend over backward for someone else. The guys that brag about having a lot of money will usually not spend it, and if they do, they'll expect much more in return. Don't ever feel compelled to do something for a lot of money if you don't want to. You're not losing money if it was never yours to begin with.

You'll hear a lot of weird shit in here. People will tell you that they murdered someone, if they were molested as a child, how many years it's been since their last erection. You'll hear business and investing secrets from intoxicated traveling businessmen, you'll be asked a lot of questions about your personal life, and it's good to have stock answers to these questions. What kind of car you drive? Okay, don't even tell me, I'll just forget that right now, whatever car you drove before the other one your boyfriend had- that's the car you drive. If someone asks me what I drive I tell them a Ford Focus, because that's what I drove in 2008. I don't need anyone looking on in the parking lot and seeing my vehicle. That way, they would know which one to follow and will see it around town. Girls have been followed home before, and girls have been attacked. I was followed one time, but I had my cell phone in my lap, called the police and lost the motorcyclists, but that's another story. Every single day a woman in our position is raped or murdered. Don't think that it can't happen to you. It's happening right now, at this moment.

Anyway, I don't want to depress you. This can be a really amazing job. You'll be praised as a goddess you'll be hugged like a mother. You'll be adored like a celebrity. You'll go to bed still buzzing with the excitement of the evening, your suitcase full of crumpled ones and your knees aching, the adrenaline still coursing through your limbs. You'll perhaps make the strangest of friends, and have the strangest of times, and experience the most honest emotions in your life thus far. You'll know your body from every angle and you'll never feel sexier as when you're bathed in the red light, captivating the room and paying all of your bills.

Anyway, that's a basic rundown. Do you have any questions for me?

Live! Nude! Girls!

Brody
San Francisco, California

I'VE NEVER BEEN one, but I hear strippers smell really nice. I hear they have fabulously slutty stage outfits. I hear they touch real cash most nights they work. I never did either of those things. I, safe in my glass case, was a live nude girl. Working at the Lusty Lady in San Francisco, CA, I didn't undress for physical dollars in my pocket at the end of the night, but I did see approximately 3000 cocks.

On my average night at the Lusty in 2001 or 2002 I arrived, careening into the club wearing zero make-up, a hoodie, and a Dickies jacket about 10 minutes before the start of my shift. I left my apartment in Russian Hill with every intention of leaving myself 15 minutes to put on my face, but after walking through the tunnel, past the edge of Chinatown and into North Beach, past all the true strip clubs with bouncers and neon (where I perceived the braver girls worked), I arrived at the Lusty with ten, maybe eight minutes to clock in and go on stage. This was less than ideal because it took time to go backstage, get my locker open, take off my clothes, choose a pair of shoes that weren't still sweaty from the day before, grab a spot at the mirror with space for my make-up bag next to three or four others, and then smoothly paint on eyeliner plus my full working girl face in a few short minutes. Usually there was a girl on the couch trying to read or close her eyes for a few minutes. No matter how it all turned out, when the clock read 10:00 PM I sprayed the soles of my shoes with rubbing alcohol (to maintain cleanliness, though about 80 different dancers per week would walk on the stage), wiped them dry, and stepped on stage.

Or stepped into the fish bowl, however you prefer to call it. I remember it shaped somewhat like a football with 12 windows downstage and a wall of floor-to-ceiling mirrors upstage. The entire floor was red carpet and there was a long, large, carpeted step that wrapped along the windowed half of the stage. There was one stripper pole at center right, but I used the smaller poles bolted on either side of most windows more frequently. There were two corner booths that had slightly larger windows than the rest, and could accommodate two people comfortably, but all the other windows opened to single-person booths with a place for the customer to drop coins to get the window to go up. There was also a completely separate work space called Private Pleasures, which was a single dancer booth, abutted by a customer booth with a bench that tightly fit two. But Private Pleasures is a whole different story for another time.

When we danced on the main stage there were many things we could not control. We couldn't change the music. We danced to whatever music was playing, although we could make requests that we might get to hear if the player's random function chose them once someone added them to the list. We couldn't control when management would be in the office (or would not be). I always preferred working when management was gone. We could not control which clients would show up at which windows or how long they would stay. We had no way of influencing who worked at what time. I feel fairly certain that fellow dancer Tiamat wanted to poke her nails into my eyes when Missy Elliot's *Work It* came on and I started bouncing up and down like a jack-in-the-box set loose. I, meanwhile, remained perplexed about the sexiest way to dance to thrash metal. Tiamat and I probably ranged from content to blissful when *Gypsy Rose Lee* by The Distillers came on, while Coco, a moonlighting librarian, would be stuck waiting for Marvin Gaye's *Sexual Healing*.

There are few things I have done with my body that felt as excellent as dancing naked for money. It was the kind of happy high that overrode complaints from my feet about five-inch platform heels. Even surrounded by mirrors, it was difficult for critical, body shaming voices to find purchase when I danced. Add two to three also-naked women to the mix and it was a special kind of magic. No two bodies looked the same, and while I was a slender, tattooed punk with a Louise Brooks bob, my floor dances never had the clean dirtiness of tall, size twelve Ginger's with her strawberries and cream complexion. If I was small, another dancer, Asia, was smaller and could work the pole as well as an actual stripper. I seriously doubt anyone else was as happy to be there as I was. In spite of the upsides, it wasn't perfect and in many ways was a just a job. I simply felt it was lucky for me there was a market for dancing naked ladies.

The question of why there was a market for dancing naked ladies at the Lusty Lady was closely tied to why it was a peepshow rather than a strip club. Think about it: a little private space for each customer, doors customers could close to each booth, and tissues on the wall; have I mentioned that yet? Live action naked women behind the window when you put money in the machine. Usually, when you deposited money, women would dance over to your window and the stage height insured you were not looking eye-to-eye no matter how short the dancer. What would you do alone in one of those booths? Permit me to elaborate on what probably seven out of ten customers did.

This is how a client interaction would begin: first, there would be the sound of a door closing. Then there would be a pause of a few minutes, during which the dancers would listen, trying to anticipate which window was about to go up. Then a window would mechanically rise. Whichever dancer was closest sauntered over and mimed a greeting with swaying hips and that come-hither glance. With the sound barriers of pounding music and the thick glass of the window, it didn't make much sense to try and talk. I remember it was always much darker in the booths than on stage, but that didn't stop me- the-dancer- from trying to see if you- the client- had your hands in your pants. If you didn't, I would try some subtle encouragement. Grab the handles at the sides of the window and do a little dip down closer. Amazingly enough, mouthing the words, "don't you want to play?" were an effective form of soundless communication.

From there it was anyone's guess what would happen next. Some guys would get this surprised look on their faces and walk away before the window even went back down. Some would just stand and watch, making no movement. Sometimes a customer would take a few moments to get his pants unzipped and then his money would run out and the window would go back down, usually prompting the dancer's response,

"Aw buddy, hope you brought more money. Can you find a bit more to get that window back up?"

I mean, they couldn't really hear you, but it was worth trying. Ideal customers would put a good amount of money in, have their pants unzipped when the window went up, and just go for it while the dancer did her thing. I believe some girls claimed they could recognize regulars (customers who visited regularly) on the main stage, but I usually couldn't. My regulars all developed in Private Pleasures, and I don't recall seeing them very often when I danced on the main stage. There seemed to be customers who regularly visited only the main stage, but few that stand out in my memory.

Dancing at the Lusty I saw many cocks, and encouraged many orgasms without ever touching a customer. Unless it was Christmas. For our holiday party the club rules changed and the dancers came out from behind the glass to give lap-dances or chat with the clients. Strangely, that didn't increase traffic much; it was a holiday after all, but we festively entertained ourselves. There was a particular frustration during a quiet shift if two or three times in a row a customer would come in, drop a minimal amount of money, and go out. To discourage this practice, management put photos of the dancers on shift up in the lobby so potential customers didn't have to make it all the way into the booth in order to see if their favorite girls were working. Some people were new to the concept of a peepshow and appeared to travel in packs. Sometimes it would be completely quiet then the door, the coins, the window rolling up and we'd see two or three dudes crowded into one booth, gesturing rudely and laughing. These times were always worse than no customers at all. Later I would learn that the most insulting human emotion is disgust. Perhaps that had something to do with the problem of those single quarter spenders.

On the other end of the spectrum, we had one older male customer who would come in and occupy one of the corner booths. He would buy out whole hours of time in that spot and I don't think a single one of us ever saw him cum. This caused a frustration of a different kind. It wasn't like he carried a sign that said "I'll never cum for you," and I know I personally tried multiple times every dirty movement or sexy enticement I could think of, to no avail, for more than an hour. Girls got to where they would give one another the heads up that it was him again, because who wants to put all that energy into an impossible cause? The thing was he would have his cock in his hands that entire time. So those were the less enjoyable and more confusing times to work, but neither the quick peeks nor the perpetual masturbator were the usual customer. The usual customer was an adult male, ready and willing to get off with the naked ladies. For the usual customer I thought it was a fun game to figure out if he was a particular fan of tits, ass, or just nudity in general. Did he seem more receptive to a naked girl's presence right up close, or was it preferable to give him some space?

Sometimes it would be a woman, and oh glory those were the best of the best times. Depending on who I was working with, an honest-to-God female presenting customer might incite a two-dancer show. On the other hand, two horny dancers could incite a two dancer show themselves, on a busy night when all the windows were flying open at a random staccato. It wasn't technically dancing anymore, being bent over Vivian's knees getting spanked, but hell. That was our stage. We could do what we wanted.

Some have written about clubs where competition between the dancers to out-hustle one another is openly encouraged. When I worked at the Lusty it was quite the opposite, and not just because we earned an hourly wage. No working situation is perfect, and the women who worked at the Lusty were often extremely independent. Some were aloof or mean, but most were open to questions and willing to pass along helpful information. The things I learned from fellow dancers backstage or even onstage covered everything from where in town to get free or low cost health care or free condoms, to how to construct a resume without listing "nude dancer" as past employment, to what the experts were saying about sex workers, to where to find and what to look for in favorite stripper shoe styles. And when the customers were mean, management was being dumb, or the night was long, the women I worked with understood. We lived through that together.

 I recall shifts when I might be dancing at stage left with Coco at stage right; a window on my side would go up, the guy would take one look at me, wait for the window to go down, and then reappear on Coco's side. Coco was about 5'2" with creamy brown skin, short dark hair, small bones and a comparatively sizable ass. Her stage presence was nurturing, almost motherly. In contrast, I am 5'7", and fairly well covered in tattoos, but my look got the occasional legit modeling gig. I may have been closer to some imaginary beauty ideal, but when it came to getting off, a customer's sincere attraction preferences came into play. At the peepshow I saw frequent evidence that some dudes are attracted to tall women, and some are attracted to short. Some to big boobs, some to big asses, and some to small feet. Pale, curly-haired, small-breasted Quinn was running her own game, which was different from big breasted, chocolate-skinned Cinnamon's and different customers responded, quite bodily, to each.

 Yet there were some commonalities. Most customers who wanted to get off responded positively when you stayed very close and watched. By leveraging your body down next to the window, with your arms up on the bars, you could create a kind of private space for a short time. Pouring out some awe and attention, arching your back, and alternating between showing him your pussy and then your face, most customers would cum. There was also a sizable contingent that preferred you to turn around and give some booty to watch. It's incredible how low you can get in super tall heels, so drop down low, eye check, see how he's doing, and if necessary drop a little lower. Second only to female customers, the male that could jiz a nice arc up onto the window held a special place in my heart. That was some delightful spontaneity. Some girls would go "Ewwww," but I always felt an element of appreciation present. As a worker, yes, the sound of coins dropping into the machines was one reason to persist at dancing. On the other hand, my personal motivation was more connected to evidence that I had aided in the gift of pleasure. That was what made a bad night decent- when I didn't feel like flirting, smiling, or being nice, and I didn't want any of those things to be a requirement for my job. It didn't have to be visible cum. Sometimes it was the look on a customer's face when she came. It was just good to know that by the virtue of semi-privacy in the club and a dancer's naked body, someone had a few moments of ecstasy in her day.

Strippers know how close to stand to a client. They know how to give lap dances, or work an open stage. The Lusty was a peepshow. My expertise was the "money shot", both given and received. Customers at the Lusty could not buy drinks and the dancers made an hourly wage. The worth of my shift was measured less by tips, and more by the length of time windows stayed open, and the number of satisfied customers passing through.

Three Little Words

Margo
Portland, Oregon

I tiptoed across his carpet to the low chair where my lip balm was stuffed in some balled-up leggings, retrieved it and swiped my lips rapidly. The THC from the delicately wrapped jointed hadn't hit me yet- not completely. "Yeah, I have this one regular customer. He wears Ray bans in the club. He's kinda creepy." I bent and crawled onto the bed where James sat in his black thermal shirt and white socks, hands folded in his jeans. The light from his fireplace flickered quietly. The room was scented with organic soy candles. "Anyway, sometimes when I give him dances, every time there is a lull in the music he leans in," -I leaned in to his ear- "and whispers, I love youuuu. I love you." The hair on the nape of James' neck flickered. I wanted to touch it. He leaned back, "He says that? Really?"

"Yeah. It's uh, creepy. And sad." I stood and stepped off the low bed, "and I've explained to him before, No you don't, you like spending time with me. You enjoy my company. You don't love me." As I mimicked this script, my voice affected the tone of a patient mother. Firm and calm, yet annoyed. "How old is he?" James asked. I thought. "Thirty-five? I don't know. He's married. He and his wife have a two year old daughter. He shows me pictures of her all the time. You'd think he'd know better than to tell me that he loves me." Those words hung in the air, awkwardly and I walked to his bathroom sink, turned the faucet and drank from it, trying not to slurp too loudly. Heart pounding. Slurp slurp thump thump. He still made me nervous, after these few years. He was suddenly behind me, when the crotch of his jeans pressed softly against my ass. He swayed. Rub rub. I wiped my wet mouth with my dry hand, and turned the faucet off. I stood and slowly turned, so that we met facing, but I kept my head low. I stood on tiptoes so that our foreheads pressed together.

And then suddenly, he turned, walked back to the bed, grabbed the remote and turned down the volume. I followed him. He was scrolling through his cell phone. I knew that he'd be heading downtown to work at the newly opened Kit Kat Club, next to the world famous Voodoo Donut. Voodoo was famous for its novelty doughnuts. Mediocre sweets with catchy names: The Ol' Dirty Bastard donut, the Tangfastic, and Butterfingering. Food Network had featured them a few times in the last decade, and there was always a line around the block. Heading there to work meant navigating the barrage of tourists. I always felt safer inside the club, despite it being located downtown and in one of the most hazardous five-block radius in the entire city.

The people were mostly walkabout downtown tourists, or accidental customers, popping in from bar, to venue, to bar, to strip club, to bar, not knowing the rules of conduct for each business, and not caring either. Customers were more likely to grope the dancers. Female customers were more catty. It was difficult to coerce the crowd to tip and not unusual for a fight to break out. Homeless people clustered in the nearby alley, waiting for donuts or change. The police circled patiently in their cars, waiting for the next outrageous act of idiocy to occur.

Last week a man had entered the Kit Kat with his pants around his ankles, and a white, lotion-like substance smeared about his genitals- which were erect, despite the frigid outdoor conditions. The bartender saw him first, and pointed, "No!" with another outstretched hand, defensively hoping to communicate her unwillingness to cope with a stranger's lubricated penis and testicles. The Bouncer had glanced over, sighed and began marching in that direction when the guy turned and ran; to where, I had no idea.

But I wasn't working tonight and here I sat, with James. Only a dozen years older than me, he'd been having sex almost as long as I'd been alive. I'd wondered about his nervous, thirteen year old self fumbling, but the now thirty eight year old man was as adept at vaginal manipulation as any dyke I'd ever known. When we fucked he was quietly confident, as with anything else. When he strolled the strip club floor in uniform, he kept his chin tucked, eyes scanning the room for any misbehavior, beneath dark furrowed eyebrows. One time I'd been hassled by a drunk man standing at my stage as I stretched from the ceiling and the walls by my ankles and thighs, my pink curls dangling beneath my inverted body. "I like your hair." The intoxicated stranger swiped at my face and I winced, not from pain or fear but from the knowledge that his filthy hand had touched me without my consent. I unhooked myself from the ceiling and landed softly on my butt, legs crossed, "Don't do that, please." He put his hand up defensively; "Oh excuse me princess, learn how to take a fucking compliment." And James was there, his eyes barely flickering, but to me the loudest thing in the club. Aesop Rock was thumping on the speakers, demanding, *"And I will remember your name and face, on the day you are judged by the Funhouse cast, and I'll rejoice in your fall from grace, with a cane to the sky like none shall pass....None shall pass, none shall pass."*

James spoke simply, 'Sir, please do not touch the dancers." Drunk guy shook his head, reached in his pocket, and retrieved a cigarette and lighter, turning to walk away from the both of us. Smoking had been outlawed in 2008, and this man probably knew that. It was an act of defiance. The audience was no longer watching me, but all heads turned to the rude stranger who had so brazenly invaded the formerly pleasant bubble of the stage. Drunky flicked his lighter. James waited two seconds, then snatched the lit cigarette with this left hand, grabbed the drunk by the collar, and marched him out of the adjacent door. When James returned he was alone and simply nodded at me once as he passed the stage, the other customers still bemused. My heart tingled. I wanted to kiss him, hug him, thank him. James was just doing his job. But in that instance he was doing it for me. "Favoritism," the other girls whispered. "That's why she gets to do whatever she wants; she must be fucking the owner," they had said. It wasn't true. It was nearly true. I was fucking the head of security.

We'd been sneaking sex for years, wise enough to hide our late night interactions from the incestuous cycle of industry gossip. I had my reasons. The stranger who had nipped me on the breast with his teeth; I punched him hard and fast, upwards in to his jaw, chipping a tooth or maybe a couple. I leapt from his lap, not bothering to gather my bra, and ran to the DJ booth. Moments later the man tore open the curtain, clutching his face and roaring through clenched jaws. James took care of it, deceptively reaching out to the man in a gracious sweeping motion of his arm, yet instead took a firm hold of him and pinched the skin the Biter's armpit, then walked him toward the exit. The man whimpered and struggled, but James was whispering fiercely- an admonition of sorts. I was still hiding behind the DJ booth, peeking over the wall as the man disappeared, led by James, out in to the rain swept streets. The DJ was bathed in the glow of the laptop, his face white and blue and solemn. He turned a switch to the stage and the lights flickered deeper red. "What was that about?"

I muttered, "He bit me in a dance. That guy bit me." The DJ sniffed and glanced at my torso and face. "Where? And why was his mouth bleeding?" But I was already stomping to the bathroom. It was empty of other women and I washed my chest in the sink, my cheeks flushed. I studied my nipple where I could not see broken blood vessels (yet), and I hoped I would not see them in the morning. James was outside of the door. "Are you okay?" He asked quietly. "He bit me." I was still holding my nipple. "I'm sorry", he spoke. And he nodded twice and turned on his heel. As I watched him go I saw Ginger and Aria whispering to each other behind their fingers, still looking at me. I hurried to the dressing room and peered out of the curtain to see that James was scribbling in the bouncer journal. Yet, I knew that he was either lying or writing nothing at all.

Customer injuries are liabilities, he explained later; I'd heard it before. *I know that you were assaulted. I'm really sorry, baby. But if the guy tries to press charges, it will come down on the dancer. That's how society works. Nobody cares about you, you're just the stripper. He's somebody's father/husband/boss.* And I knew that he was right. And that was the nature of our relationship. He protected the club, he protected the other dancers, and he protected me.

It was close to the beginning of the start of the evening shift and I knew that he would depart soon. I would return home to my quiet apartment. Scroll through Facebook. Do some sit-ups. Make a grocery list for tomorrow's Whole Food's trip. I'd rather be in his bed. I sighed, more to myself than I realized. James was still looking at his phone. But now, James was looking at the screen a bit longer than usual. He frowned. "A shooting at Mystic." I sat up. "What?" He replied, "I guess there was a shooting at Mystic just now. That's all I know." I didn't ask who had sent the text message; bouncers and dancers and cooks and management intermingled so much that we all knew each other anyway, or knew of each other. I found my cell in the sheets, and tapped tapped tapped in to the Google window. We looked at news articles in silence for a couple minutes, but it didn't offer much. Two injured. Updated. Four injuries. Shooter in custody. No names. I wondered about my friends there.

The pot was kicking in, and my brain was riding it in waves and crashes. This shit was strong, and I was new to weed. I wondered how many seconds had passed or if they had actually been minutes. I looked at the clock over my shoulder, not realizing my cell phone was still glowing its information at my face. Then forgetting that thought, I realized the time hadn't changed. 8:21. James reclined in the bed, onto his back And stared at the ceiling. He rolled over to face me, chewing his lip, thinking. A wave of vibration ran throughout my brain and I knew that the nearly legal drugs were doing their job. "You want to play with my boobs?"

"Sure. Yes. I would love to." He paused, and I think he expected me to pull the sweater over my head, but rather I took his hands in my fingers and pressed them against my belly. He fumbled with the blue fabric until he reached underneath and slid his palms against my skin. My pectoral muscles were always sore from the repetitive pole acrobatics I performed three times a week, but he wasn't touching those. He wouldn't know to- he wasn't a stripper- but he was focused. He furrowed his brow in stoned concentration, pushing my areolas up and around and together and apart. I watched his hands, switching focus from his face to his fingers. I leaned down, and smelled his face. His scent was my favorite thing, more favored than his strong, clean hands, or lean waist, or dry, quiet sense of humor. I loved his scent more than his short, dark hair, or his cold grey eyes.

I wondered what he loved about me, if anything. He was kissing me. Spikes of facial hair bit into my soft, already chapped lips, but I pressed harder against him, and felt my tongue relax against his. I tasted his mouth, and my heart shuddered. We were beginning a dance of sorts that I knew would end with me hugging his side while he fiddled with his text messages. I pulled my mouth from his and pulled my v neck sweater over my head, my short, pink hair fluffing about my face. I reached for him again and he rolled me on to my back, our mouths never leaving each others. His belt was down, and I was frantically pulling at him, I knew that his cock would taste like clean, soapy meat and that he would fuck my face as I gasped happily. His fingers grasped at the hips of my leggings and they were stretched around my thighs as he put two fingers to my lips, wetting them in my mouth before pressing against my clitoris, rubbing in circles. He was so good at sex.

I moved with him to my back and lifted my knees to encourage him to enter me, and he did, his mouth falling agape. I felt all the cylindrical walls of my vagina pulsate in waves, and then imagined that the walls became square and then triangular, and then I pressed my fingers, palms, arms and skin and bones against his back, warm with sweat, and I loved him and I loved him and I loved him and Ray Bans was suddenly whispering in my brain, "I love you." I shook my head, kissed the side of James' face frantically as he moaned and his mouth found mine, but again I felt the jagged fingernails of Ray Bans on the nape of my neck as his whispered to me in that curtained small room, "I love you. I love you." I shook my head once again and pulled my fingers to James' face, sliding his slick hair backward and in to my fists. We were moving like water. The only sounds came from our breath and the sporadic droplets of rain that fell outside. He fucked me hard into the bed, I rubbed the length of his back and shoulders as I squirmed in circles onto his cock, the wetness slapping against us both.

He tucked his chin to kiss between my breasts, and the voices of a dozen strangers echoed in my ears, "Hey, puffy nipple girl. You have puffy nipples." I coughed to clear their voices away, with a sweeping motion of my lungs, and my brain was still for a moment; it was only James and I. He was moving inside me still and I was grateful for it. My right hand reached to encircle the width of him and I felt a slickness between us that was shocking. "Oh my God," he gasped, and nodded. He felt it too. Wet wet, slap slap. I wondered what a spider thought of the silky, stretching thread that she pulled from her body to build a web- a snare; f she thought of it at all, or if she knew how much she relied upon the substance. He pulled his weight to me and reached to my neck cupping my face in his hands, our foreheads pressed together so hard that I felt his brain throbbing in rhythm to his cock. I was choking on the heat of his breath and I came and I came and I came.

And we were still, but for our inhales and exhales. James pulled from me and was on his back, patting my leg: one, two, three. I heard nothing except breathing. The faces of my customers loomed over us, smiling. "You sure have a real tight pussy." Grinned the face of the biker, I called him Santa Claus. I was angry. I was angry at the men not in the room. I wondered what Ray Bans was doing now. Having dinner with his wife, perhaps. Putting their daughter to bed. I could never tell him. But I'd see him soon, and stare at his face. He had denied me happiness and didn't even know it. I suddenly wanted to cry, and coughed in to my hand to stifle the tears. James was absentmindedly running his fingers over his wet stomach. He took a deep breath. In the candle light I saw his head turn. "You know- I wanted to tell you something. Just now. But.your customer ruined it." Silence. It wasn't just me. Four years of sex, and yet I'd managed to be denied the only thing I'd wanted to be told. I groaned, covering my face with a hand. He laughed, and kissed my fingers. "I love you." I told him. He didn't blink at all, yet the corners of his mouth arched up into the crinkles of his eyes. "I love you too, Emma." I turned and pushed my face in to the pillows, so that he couldn't see the tears in my eyes and the grin on my lips. Tap tap tap on his cell phone. Quiet. Then I jumped.

"Shot in the head. Their bouncer was shot in the head." His voice trailed off. I hadn't worked at Mystic in months, and I wondered which man had been attacked. They had all been very nice men- quiet, efficient. I didn't know any of them very well, but I didn't want to think that any of them were dead. "I don't want you to go to work." I squeaked. He shook his head, "I'll be fine. I'm sure it's an isolated incident, or some gang shit." He set his phone down. But,

I saw him blink twice, thinking. Considering what it might be like to die at work, maybe. I sat up and reached for a glass of water. It was empty. I stared at it stupidly until he took it from my hand, stood on the bed to step to the floor, the sink, and eventually to the faucet. He looked at himself in the mirror. No expression. For a moment I wondered if he'd forgotten I was there. I looked away, suddenly hit with the feeling that I should be getting dressed to leave.

He climbed back in bed, held the glass to me, and I reached in silence to drink from it, wiping my mouth with my fingers, which were still scented from both our bodies. I handed it back to him. My eyes were low beneath my heavy bangs. "This shit is strong." He raised an eyebrow and looked at the glass, "What?" I laughed, nearly snorting. "The pot. The marijuana is strong. I'm really- I'm really high." He smiled with closed lips, his eyes softening for only a moment. I squirmed to cover my body beneath the blankets. "Do you like your job?" I suddenly realized that I'd never asked him before.

He rubbed his chin. Offered the glass again, I waved it away. He set it on the glass table beside us. "I love my job. Sure, there are rough nights. You know that. I get bored too. I get angry. But it's a job. Some of the people will really ruin it for you. It's hard not to hate them. The adrenaline is like nothing else. You and I both have stories. We get to see things most people can't even imagine. I guess, I don't know. When something like this happens, I wonder what is sacrificed. I wonder if I've sacrificed anything, by not having a normal job. Who knows? But at least I get to meet a lot of interesting people. Like you." He smiled again, his head cocked to one side. I thought of all the backrubs, unwanted cheek kisses, confessions of obsession, and mutterings of admiration. The words that meant nothing more than the money attached to them. I sighed.

He reached under my belly, between my legs. He moaned quietly, initiating the understanding in me that he was ready to make me come again. I was shocked that his fingers weren't exhausted. I loved him, at that moment, despite myself. He pressed his weight on top of me, and I felt his nipples and chest hair connect with my back. His right hand found my clitoris as his cock entered me again, and he fucked and rubbed me as I felt my eyes squeezing shut in complete fullness. And yet, I wondered what I had sacrificed.

Silver Lining

Sterling
Portland, Oregon

Sometimes when it's slow, and all there is this cold endless abyss of a room, I push my cunt against the pole and stare up at the vaulted ceiling and I imagine that 16 foot pole is my cock, that I have the biggest cock in the world. I get lost in my thoughts about how gender defines us and what it would have been like if I was a well endowed man, what might have been instead. I lay there and get lost in my thoughts to the slow melodic music that I always play, even though everyone knows that Elliott Smith and Coco Rosie don't belong at the strip club.

However, they belong at my strip club. They belong to me when I am on stage dreaming and analyzing what is and what isn't and every minute decision that I've ever made, which has brought me to exactly this moment. It seems depressing, and it is, but maybe that's part of what I love best about it all- about the sex industry and this world of which I am now so very familiar. The intensity. The naked truths and the bold-faced lies all jumbled together under one roof. It takes a great sense of intuition to be able to tell the two apart. I have gotten to a point where my ability to see through people's bullshit has gotten pretty fine tuned. Of course, I've been wrong before, with dire emotional consequences, particularly when I've been wrong about girls at work, when I've let my guard down and was lied to, as well as about. Truth is, I'm a tender thing. A blessing and a curse in this line of work.

Late December at the titty-bar is a particularly glum time, especially for dancers. It was Monday. I was scheduled to work the mid shift at Casa Diablo and I was cutting it close to being late, as traffic was stopped dead on the Fremont Bridge. There are few feelings comparable to those that erupt within oneself whilst being stuck on a bridge in the pouring rain. I knew the DJ would be setting up for the shift, and I called him to say that I probably wouldn't make it in time. He said there was a jumper and that was what was holding up traffic; he saw an update on Facebook that the bridge was shut down while the cops tried to talk down this guy from taking his own life. Really puts my strife about being late into perspective.

I ended up being merely five minutes late, decided to go bare faced, shed my leggings, and dance in the over-sized John Lennon shirt & beat up oatmeal colored cardigan that I wore in to the club that day. Pulled on some white cotton panties, my ballet flats and was ready to go. Stripper casual: a look that would be unacceptable for strippers in most other parts of the country, but was applauded here in Portland. I love being a stripper. I love starting my day off dancing to Bjork or Tom Waits, and "bashfully" revealing my cunt to what very well could be one of my dad's friends. I love never having to lie, or never having to apologize for walking away when I feel like it. I love selling a product that I believe in more than anything- myself.

Some days, though, are dreadful. In any industry there will be bad days but to me, the bad days as a stripper really are just dreadful. This particular Monday was shaping up to be just that. It was turning out to be the kind of day where it felt like every touch from every customer was tainted with a layer of filth, infecting me, searing my very being, making it impossible for me to ever wash myself clean again. Every compliment was coated in sarcasm, every rejection thick and palpable.

A group of vegan women came in "just to try the food"; they came in for the novelty of a vegan strip club. They were staring, not tipping, and loudly pointing out any flaw they believed a dancer onstage possessed. The blue collar working stiffs- the only tipping customers at the rack, covered in grease, licking their teeth, spitting black chew remnants into their empty beer mugs, were only producing dollars if we spread our pussies open "real wide", as well as on demand. The regulars, holding down the bar, massaging the girls' shoulders upon request but never spending any real dough because, "they don't pay for lap dances". Then, to top it all off, the only one who'd bought any dances from me today was Doug. He's been in maybe five other times. He only spends money on me. He comes to see me, specifically. He wants me to call him daddy. He wants me to let him choke me. He wants to pinch my nipples so hard I tear up. I let him. I'm not even sure why I let him. It's so slow, and I'm so bored, and I haven't even made my house fee. I'm floating above myself, watching it happen. He had this look on his face like he thinks he's really bringing me pleasure. It's all I can do to make it through one song. He asks me for another dance, and I tell him no. That's enough of that.

I'm in the bathroom, letting some tears come out of my body. When I cry at work, I like to lean forward and allow the tears to drip right out of my eyes and onto the floor, without ever touching my skin, so that they make perfect little round drops. It distracts me from my sadness. It feeds my OCD. I begin to care more about getting them into a perfect, straight row of teardrops than anything else. This little crying game of mine helps to ensure that I won't spend too much time weeping. I hate being caught in tears by other girls. It's not that my coworkers are mean, they are actually mostly very kind and care for my well being. It's just that when they ask what's wrong I don't ever know how to answer. It's never just one thing I can truly point out. It's this feeling of being drained and depleted. It's feeling lousy about feeling lousy. It's loving what I do so much that my heart is on the brink of bursting, and then hating it so much the next moment, that I become riddled with confusion and have no explanation to offer anyone who might inquire about what it is that ails me.

The rest of the day was pretty routine, after the groups of insufferable creatures from earlier eventually made their way out of the club. There was a steady stream of clientele, some just fine, some simply intolerable. Luckily my best friend was the bartender that day, so at least I had someone to roll my eyes with. My BFF is maybe as strange a bird as I. Her name is Zorpicon;

she has pastel pink hair, shaved only above her ears and the back of her head. She's covered in trash polka tattoos and has "love is vile" scrolled across her fingers. With all this being said, she's also one of the prettiest girls you're ever likely to meet in person. Oh, and she's super into taxidermy, which brings me to the interesting part of my day. But before I get ahead of myself, let me back up a bit.

The shift was finally over. We were headed out the door of Casa into our prospective vehicles. We would later convene at one of our favorite eateries for the biggest plate of nachos that one might be able to procure at such an hour. She pulled out of the driveway before me. I followed her, but stopped at the convenience store down the street for a pack of smokes. As I was getting back into my car I noticed I had left my door unlocked, which wasn't like me. I thought nothing of it- until I pulled out of the parking lot, flipped on my radio, and then heard a voice come from my back seat.

"I never woulda thought you for a Ford girl." It was Doug. My heart dropped into my stomach. Fuck. This is how I die. Or. Maybe not. When I got in my car I had left my phone on my lap. I pushed the send button and it started calling my last contact. Zorpicon. I prayed she would pick up and listen in on the conversation."Don't be scared, baby. Daddy just wanted to tuck you in tonight."

"Doug. This isn't okay. This is terrifying. I'm going to pull over, and you are going to get out of my car."

"If you pull over I'm going to shove my pocket knife into your throat. You don't want that, do you?

"I can't drive forever."

"We won't. Go to your place. We're gonna have some fun, just you and me."

I was scared. I didn't respond. Instead, I cried. I sobbed the whole way there. I considered driving to the police station, and I changed my course."Where are you going, girl? You think this is the first time I've followed you? TURN AROUND." Fuck. This is it, then. I couldn't have felt more trapped. When we were almost to my place, I noticed my phone light up and say "call ended

10 min 18 sec," which means she answered. I prayed she heard what was happening.

When we got there, He instructed me to exit the car and stand there with my hands to the side awaiting directions. I shook my head, so he knew I heard him. I sucked in some air and wiped my face. I can do this. I got out of the car. So did he. He didn't ask for my keys. Big mistake Doug, big mistake. He turned towards me and grabbed my face hard and started to kiss me. I had positioned the keys in my clenched fist and stabbed him in the ribs. Hard. He yelped, gripped his thick fingers to my throat then started choking me. Also hard. Maybe harder than I had stabbed him. Fuck. I was beginning to see stars and feel faint. I struggled for breath and beat my fists against him.

Out of nowhere, blood spurted from his mouth, his eyes grew wide and his hands relaxed around my neck. He slumped his whole weight on to me and I fell over. I screamed and pushed him off. Zorpicon. She was standing over us with a bloody knife in her hand and a wild look in her eyes. In a beat we were dragging him, gargling his own blood, half alive, his breathing weighted, to our basement, where Zorpy kept her Taxidermy collection. "I've always wanted human bones!" she exclaimed, that same wild look in her eyes, and a splatter of blood on her cheek.

Well, I guess we finally figured out how to "collect customers."

Marilyn

Lily Fury
New York

*A*IN'T NOTHIN' HERE *for you girl. Ain't never was.* The elements become sleepy, become fluid. *This is the world of nowhere,* he says, *and you're going nowhere fast.* Bill, My schizophrenic roommate tells me this every early morning when I'm sticky from the sweat and the heroin withdrawal, counting crumpled bills on his coffee table as the sun rises just one more time. He looks like Einstein with his wild hair and crazy eyes. He says he's in some witness protection program because he used to be in the CIA. He gets institutionalized on a yearly basis. I'm keeping crumpled bills in stacks in this fifties heart shaped suitcase I stole from Goodwill. When the time's right I'll make a run for it. *Blue heart needs resurrection,* I think as I sleep here in clouds of smoke, burning for something new, something past this nothingness, this loss of stimulation; and this sky full o' stars just don't cut it anymore and hasn't for weeks now.

    I listen to Bill talk all manic-like about conspiracy theories he swears he's witnessed. I fall asleep listening to them. Conspiracy theories have become my bed time stories. I awake to banging on the door. Bill is already up and ready for his clientele. We are both hustlers, just of different trades. He sells pounds of marijuana to subsidize his crazy check. I don't pay Bill rent. I think he just likes having me around as the eye candy, as the crazy stranger girl in this nowhere town. He calls me Marilyn Monroe. I look nothing like her with my red wild hair and pale skin but I think he reflects that our personalities were somehow similar, both beautiful and crazy he says, both beautiful and broken. Sometimes his friends give me rides to the club and sometimes my friend Bridget does. Bridget more or less got me the job. She has a celestial halo of blonde hair and we are both chasing the dragon. I'm still 17. The manager at the club had never even asked to see my ID, only for me to strip for him in his sleazy office while he jerked off.

I walk to the shower and see the bruises I keep accumulating dancing around that pole, but the truth is, I never have felt so alive as the nights that I swing around that pole like some sort of manic pixie. I love the sensation of stepping onto the stage and having their eyes watch me; "entertain me" their eyes whisper, "seduce me" and I do. I let the water run over me, washing off my beautiful "sins" from the previous night. The water is like therapy to my body and I fall into a daydream of sorts...

He is above me, filthy, sweaty and lawless, devoid of ethics or morals; he is all about self-satisfaction. I was a young girl, 12 to be exact. It's dark in my small room in which he has invaded once again. Sleeping has become problematic as this becomes more and more of a routine for him. I try to close my eyes at night but instead I lay still and petrified, watching for movements outside my bedroom door, praying that maybe he has forgotten about me tonight. I had averted his eyes all day. I have stopped talking back to him or attempting to protect my mother from his rage. I am the silent girl that I assume he wants me to be, but this is not good enough for him. Perhaps until I am dead, nothing will be good enough for him. He dry fucks me, bruising my skin while he holds me down rubbing his hard erection between my legs. It's simulated fucking- not exactly rape, but for my spirit it feels close enough. I wait for the wetness to leak through my pajamas or his pants, if he is wearing them.

Then he will get up to leave, but this is when the threats and terrorizing occur, This is when he puts his 9 millimeter to my head and swears he will kill me and my mother if I ever tell. I fearfully promise I won't. I want to ask him why. I want to tell him I'm sorry for whatever I did. But, I know these attempts will prove futile as they have in the past, so I just pray for the quickness, to get it over with as fast as possible. Promises are just air to him so he strikes me with his hand, marking my thighs or back with welts and bruises. He knows not to hit me where someone might see. He is smart and it seems like maybe he has done this before. I yelp a little but try to not so much because I've noticed that the more I cry, the more he gets off on it and won't stop, maniacally taking swings at me until I scream so loud that I break his malicious trance and he stops for a second. He smiles before he leaves- the terrorist's smile of accomplishment.

"Lily! Lily!" Bill yells at me. There's blood streaming down the drain of the shower and I'm not sure where it's coming from. The sun is leaking in through the windows. He shuts the water off and puts a towel to my head. "What the fuck happened here?" he asks. "I don't know, I must have hit my head," I tell him. He inspects my head. He told me once that he used to help bandage soldiers in Vietnam. "You scared the shit out of me kid, but it's not a big cut, I think you'll be okay, just be more careful." I promise him that I will be and he notices the tears welling up in my eyes. The memories just get more and more intense. I wonder how much longer I will have to live with them. "Hey, you okay? C'mon you rock star, you're okay kid, right?" I half smile at his determination for me as I take his hand to steady myself from the shower. He carries me into the bedroom and starts singing songs to me. "Hey Bill" I start. "Yes, Lily?" he answers. "I love you fucker," I tell him. He smiles exposing all of his yellow and rotting teeth, but then there's another knock on the door. "I love you always you rock star Marilyn Monroe," he says to me as he leaves the room to go conduct business.

I pack my little heart shaped suitcase with lingerie and dancewear for tonight. It's Friday and our club should be packed. I hear a car horn honking in the driveway. Is it almost 5:00 already? Bill peeks his head in and tells me that Bridget is waiting for me. I grab my little suitcase, peck Bill on the cheek and run outside into the blinding sunlight. Bridget's windows are rolled down and she's blasting music. I get in and look at her; she doesn't look so well. She keeps sniffing and her eyes are watery, first signs of dope sickness. She throws me her cell phone and asks if I can make a call for her so we can get through tonight. We pick up our dope and drive down the lone highways to make it to our shift in time. We work at one of two strip clubs in this nowhere state of Vermont. The florescent sign to our white trash strip club flickers in the sunset.

Me and Bridget both get out our tools and fix in the car. I hold my breath as I push down on the plunger of my syringe, watch the blue swim over my pupils in the rearview mirror and feel the euphoria rising. "Fuck!" Bridget yells. Her arm is a brutalized, bloody mess. She just started shooting up so she hasn't quite gotten the hang of it yet. "Hey, calm down blondie, I got you." I appease her and pull the tourniquet a little harder around her arm, "Hey Bridget," I say as I inspect her arm until I see a vein pop. "What, love?" she answers. "Is there anything from your past that haunts you," I finally ask as I pull blood back in the syringe, push down and watch the rush ride over her as she falls into a slight and content nod. I take out some cover up and start rubbing it over her track marks. "Yes" she whispers finally; "Why?"

I had suspected as much. Me and her were both born into something a little too crazy, and left to deal with the consequences, regardless. "Well what do you do to fix it?" I ask. She holds up an empty bag of dope and replies, "this shit works pretty well in blocking it all out even if it's not a permanent fix." I sigh. Of course she doesn't know the answers either. I want to ask her what she is blocking out but, I don't want to pry too much or get too heavy before we traipse into the land of the artificial smiles. She opens my door for me and we walk into the club together hand in hand, but before we enter she whispers in my ear, "Hey, when I know the answer, I promise I'll let you know too."

I smile at her as we walk to the dressing room to put on our outfits. "Oh great, she's here!" I hear my nemesis "Jade" whining to her white trash stripper cohorts about me. I smile up at them letting them know I've heard them and they scatter and disperse like rats. I pick out a glittering red sequined bikini that matches my red hair, and then put on big black pleather boots that come up to my thighs. I hear my name announced by the DJ, enter the stage, and dance with wild and reckless abandon. My stripper alter ego, Ruby, is always smiling, always joyous. When Ruby emerges each night in this club life becomes just one big adventure all the time. She is completely in love with and enchanted by the world around her, how beautiful it is to live her/be her five nights a week, to not have a care in the world, and to own her laugh and her vibrancy.

I hit the floor after working up a sweat and walk to the bar, where I see two men I've never seen here before engaging in what seems like serious conversation. I wait for the seriousness in their faces to cease to approach them but just as I sit down, one of the men leaves. "Are you here for business?" I ask him. He smiles at me and then looks at the bartender, "Get uh…" he stutters, waiting for me or our bartender Caty to intervene. "Ruby," Caty replies, smiling up at him and me. I smile back. "Get Ruby whatever she likes." he responds with a smile. Caty is one of the younger and cooler bartenders that will actually serve me alcohol. "One Jack and Coke coming up," she says, and then leans in towards me while delivering it to me. "This is Rob; he's new around here. Be careful around him. His friend who just left, I overheard him talking pretty crazy. I know you can take care of yourself but just a heads up," she whispers and then winks at me. "Girl talk?" he asks leaning in closer. "Always," I tell him.

"So what's your story? I've never seen you around here," I say, changing the subject. He looks away momentarily as if thinking of the right response or wondering if he can trust me. "Yeah, I'm new in town. I live a few blocks away for now anyway," he says. "And what are your plans?" I ask him. He has an air of mystery about him that I want to break open. He has striking deep brown eyes, a goatee on his symmetrical face and dirty blonde hair that runs a little past his ears. He looks like he could be in his mid to late twenties. He eventually shrugs my question about his plans. "Show me your scars," I whisper to him, "and I'll show you mine." He laughs and I throw back my shot, take his hand in mine and lead him with me through the parade of people and flashing lights. He has a suit on that looks expensive, and looks like he's dying to get out of. His confidence is sexy; he walks without fear.

"How much?" he asks, as we approach the private dance booths. "That depends on how long you want me for," I reply, smiling. "How about all night?" he asks. I laugh and tell him that can be done, and I tell one of the bouncers that I need the champagne room. "Just you two?" he asks. The champagne room is usually reserved for groups of men and more than one dancer at its cost. "I don't know," I respond looking at Rob; "What do you think of her?" I ask while eyeing Bridget, who is hard at work hustling on the floor talking to some regular. Two girl dances with Bridget are fun because I have chemistry with her, and we always try to sell each other to the new clients who seem to have cash to spare. "She's hot," he says. "She is." I gush, and head to the floor to grab her. "But hey," he says, stopping me; "I want some alone time with just you." It's sweet the way he says it, almost chivalrous, and I almost stumble, forget where I am and how I'm supposed to be hustling these guys my hardest like Bridget trained me; *Don't think of them as humans, they are just here to pay us and that's it.*

I nod at him. I run to the floor to grab Bridget who is chatting with a regular. "Hey beautiful," I smile at her. "Hey," she smiles back. I pull her towards me, "I have this guy, loaded, wants a two girl show in the champagne room, and you probably shouldn't pass this up," I tell her. She laughs. "Definitely not, and Jimmy here was only going to buy one dance I'm sure, and you know how he tries to draw it out." she rolls her eyes. "Hey Jimmy, Can you wait here for me?" she asks him. We both know Jimmy isn't going anywhere and will be here all night. Jimmy smiles and nods. I grab Bridget's hand with a girlish squeal and we prance back over to the champagne room. "So who is this mystery man?" she asks as we approach the door. "I don't know but he's hot and he seems like he's got money to spend."

The bouncer informs us that he's already paid for both of us for an hour, and he's inside waiting next to the mini bar as we hit the small stage together. He relaxes and watches contently as we undress each other slowly, take turns with an ice cube, and drizzle it all over our warm dancing bodies. She playfully spanks me and I let out a sigh. We kiss and move seductively closer to him until we are right up close to him and before I know it, the show is about to end. He tips her in four hundreds; she kisses him and me on the cheek as I walk her to the door on the way out. "Thanks for that, girl, I needed it. You know I got you next time. Hey, just so you know though and this could be bullshit, you know how rumors start in these nowhere towns but look at him;

he doesn't belong here. Word on the street is that he's on the run or something," she says while looking back at him before exiting the room.

Now it's just me and Rob. My heart is pulsing; his energy draws me to him and I have to remember to keep my game face on and keep Ruby in full gear. "That was really sexy," he tells me. I smile. "You liked it?" I ask. "Oh yeah," he answers, "I like you." I spit back, "you don't know me," before I know what I'm saying, but it's too late, and the cautious Lily is out of her cage. "Well what I do know, I like, is that okay with you?" he asks, taking my hand in his and kissing it delicately. I blush. I gyrate my hips on his lap and put his hands around my waist. I'm starting to sweat and can imagine he must be getting hot in here so I take his suit jacket off for him, but before he can protest I feel that outline of a gun holster in his belt line. So that's why he never took his jacket off. "You said you live a few blocks from here," I say. "I do," he responds. "So what are you afraid of?" I ask. "Nothing," he says almost defiantly. He gets up and makes himself and me a drink. I do my shot and eye him, wanting to unlock his story, his secrets. "Hey, I'll pay you a thousand dollar tip if you split this joint with me." He can tell I'm thinking about it. We aren't supposed to leave with customers but I'm sure I could get Bridget to cover for me. "Wait for me outside in the parking lot," I tell him, and he exits the room.

I go to collect my cut from the bouncer and wait for Bridget to be done with her dance with Jimmy to talk to her. "Hey, I'm leaving- cover for me if anyone asks. Tell them I got sick or something." She nods and wipes the sweat off my head. "Don't make me come looking for you, and seriously call at any hour if you need a ride home, but I hope he's paying you good money." She kisses my cheek. I quickly change in the dressing room and try to go unnoticed until I get into the parking lot. He's sitting on a Harley. I smile excitedly and jump on the back, he hands me a helmet, and we ride together down these nowhere streets. I put my arms around him and feel exhilarated with the wind in my face, racing down these obscure and forgotten streets, and when we stop I don't want to. I want to keep going and ride far away from this remote hell, and be transported into a portal of a world where I can feel free every day.

I follow him to a small apartment in a lonely and decrepit looking apartment building. Inside there is a table and two chairs, a mattress, and two suitcases still packed by the door. He hasn't been here for long it seems, or maybe he needs to keep his stuff packed in case he has to leave with little notice? He removes his jacket and his button down shirt and he has some amazing artwork tattooed into his muscular arms. I find myself in the arms of the dangerous stranger in town. I can hear Bill ridiculing me from here; "Crazy rock star bitch, you want to die," he would say. I fall into his arms and he's taking big swigs of a bottle of whiskey, I take small sips in between his gulps wanting to remember this night. He asks about my life. I tell him there's not too much to tell; I grew up in this wasteland of a state, was put into foster care at 12, and hit the road a couple years ago. Traveled the East coast to down south, to the West coast and back again. He looks almost sad for me.

I ask about him. He tells me he has a daughter and he shows me a photo of a smiling blonde toddler. I tell him she's beautiful. He tells me he's working a construction job down the street from here for now, but that he's from California. I ask him if he's in some sort of witness protection program and he laughs. He tells me he grew up in foster care mostly as well. "Well isn't that cute," I say laughing. "A match made in white trash heaven." We both laugh, and then kiss, and I urge him to drink more. I need some sort of liquid truth spilling from this guy before I decide whether to lie down next to him or split. It's never smart to fall for potential clients, but I can't help the feelings arising in my stomach. Outside the window the sky is black. I can see whole constellations through the dust in the sky. I think about how one action can change the entire course of your life and as the bottle empties, the stories start flowing. He makes me swear to secrecy and I do.

He got into selling guns when he was a teenager- him and a few of his close friends. He's done two years in prison, he's only been in love once, with his daughter's mother, but she wanted him to go legal with everything. He had a hard time adjusting to a life he never knew, a 9-5 job and all that bullshit, so he continued his life of crime. They split and things got out more and more out of control back in Cali. He didn't specify who, but that there were people looking for him, and he has to wait for the dust to settle to go back out to Cali. He's slurring his words now. I rub his back, take his boots off, and put the sheets over him on his bed. He looks up at me before he falls into a deep sleep and tells me I'm beautiful and to not leave, not tonight, and I promise him I won't. He seems satisfied with that because he closes his eyes and his breathing deepens.

I look around the suspiciously empty room. There's nothing except for what I initially saw coming in, so I go into the bathroom to wash my face and see a side closet in the bathroom. There's a safe up top with an array of guns in it, three different state I.D.'s with his face on them with three different birth dates and identities, one passport, a notepad with a list of names, numbers and some prices next to the names, with some of the names crossed off and some not. I dig deeper and find a tattered copy of Vladimir Nabokov's *Lolita*, one of my favorite books. I hadn't pegged him for a literary type but wasn't surprised either. I lift up the heavy book to read the words again but a picture falls out, and then another one.

The photos are of men with gunshot wounds; staged? No, these aren't staged. These men are dead. They are blindfolded so I can't see much of their face or their eyes, but they are real, they are corpses, and chills run down my back. Somehow I wonder if I should make that call right about now for my girlfriend to pick me up, put his stuff neatly back in his safe and return to the room to get my things. I open my cellphone but then I remember my promise about not leaving without saying goodbye, and I still hadn't collected my $1,000 yet. But, I also wasn't sure I'd be sleeping next to a murderer. Maybe if I could just have some justification of why he has them those photos, or why he killed those men- those nameless, faceless men- that I will never be able to forget now. I drop my cell phone and crawl into bed with him. He wraps his arms around me and it occurs to me that I'm sleeping in the arms of a killer, but haven't felt so safe in a long time, if ever. I drift off to sleep holding his wrists in my hands.

I'm falling and I open my mouth to scream but nothing comes out. My childhood bedroom door is shaking and the locks are slowly breaking, unable to withstand the force behind them. I know it's only a matter of seconds before the invasion begins again. With brutal force the door tears down and he puts his hands around my neck to choke out my screams that have finally surfaced. "There's nobody here to hear your cries," he whispers laughing. I can't breathe and I try to bite him, but he only laughs again and rips off my pajama shirt. I'm terrified as he defiles me. I am a prisoner in my own bedroom. I am so weak. I promise myself that one day I will hurt him the way he's hurt me. One day he will know my pain, live with it, and die with it.

"Ruby!" I hear a voice call out from the depths of somewhere. I'm in that in-between world of dreams and reality where the dream world still feels so real. Rob is shaking me awake with a look of true concern on his face. I look up at him and tell him I'm okay. "You sure?" he asks, "cause you freaked me the fuck out. What is it? What were you dreaming about?" I look away from him. There's rain beating against the windows and the roof. "I have P.T.S.D.," I tell him, "It happens most nights." He looks contemplative. I try to fight back the tears but between the slight hangover and morning dope sickness, the tears come anyway. He cradles me. "Did somebody hurt you?" he asks me, and tells me I was talking in my sleep. I just nod and try to wipe the tears away. I get up and put my boots on. "Hey thanks for last night but I have to run so can you pay me what you owe me so I can go?" I ask him. "Yeah, I mean of course," he says, counting out hundreds and handing them to me. He holds my face in his hand and looks me in the eyes; "But please don't go. It's raining outside and I'm making coffee and just please don't go. I want to get to know you more and you're the prettiest and craziest little thing I've met in a while," he says. His face softens, he smiles, and adds that last night he was genuinely the happiest he'd been in a long while. "It was nice to meet you," I say, and stubbornly walk out into the rain and put my thumb out when I get to the main road. I can feel his eyes watching me but don't care. Fuck Ruby. Fuck everything. I am not her. I am broken and nobody can fix me. A car pulls to the side of the road and takes me back to Bill's.

I get out and run inside past Bill. "Hey, no 'good morning?' I was worried sick about you, you crazy bitch," he says, looking up from his bong and the smoke that surrounds him and his buddies. He goes back to talking them into a higher price for the weed. "This is primo shit," I can hear him saying to his customers from the tiny bedroom. I fix up my needle with two times the amount of dope I usually take to get off, plunge it all into my arm, and fade far, far away from this room, from this cluttered apartment, from all the memories and the nightmares and into the clouds and deep into oblivion. The next night I'm back at the club again. I never made it back in Saturday. I woke up in the hospital from an overdose and got an earful from Bill. Tonight I'm back in action and although I'm not quite positive yet, I have a suspicion of what I might be able to do to make the nightmares stop.

I hit the floor after exiting the stage and smile at the crowd. A regular comes up and asks for a private dance. I smile and lead him to the booths. When I get there I'm shocked to see Rob standing there. He's dressed casually- not in a business suit this time- and has a look of urgency when he sees me. He asks if he can talk to me. I tell him I have a customer and I don't have time to talk, but he pushes and tells me he'll make it worth my time. I make him wait until I'm done in the private booth with my regular, then lead him into the booth and start dancing for him. "You don't have to do that. I just want to talk," he says. "You weren't here last night," he adds. "So now you're checking up on me?" I almost laugh. "I was worried when you left so abruptly," he says. "Well I'm a big girl," I tell him. "Don't worry about me."

"That's not what your friend said last night," he replies. I look at him quizzically and then it hits me, Bridget, that fucking bitch, she must have told him that I overdosed. "She did, did she?" I ask. "Yeah, that and a few other choice words, and to stay away from you," he adds. I half smile. "Listen- when you get off work, I'll be out front on my bike," he says. He doesn't wait for me to answer, just tips me with a few hundreds and disappears. I think of the photographs while getting dressed at the end of the night. I think about how I'd love for my stepfather to end up like the men in the photos.

At the end of the night I walk to the parking lot with Bridget, both of us tired from being on our feet all night. I see him on his motorcycle next to her car, waiting for me with an extra helmet in his hands. "Please tell me that you're not leaving with him," she says protectively. "I'll be fine," I tell her. She snaps her gum in disapproval. "Listen," I tell her, "he had nothing to do with last night. I just went a little overboard. I'll be okay." She rolls her eyes but holds her arms out to hug me. "Don't fucking scare me like that again you little bitch," she says, and then reminds me to call her to come pick me up whenever I need her. She flashes Rob a menacing glare and drives away. I get on his bike and we drive back to his house.

He takes a chair out for me to sit down at his table and I do. He sits down too. There's a bottle of whiskey on the table and two shot glasses; he pours me a shot and then himself one. There's nothing romantic in the air; it feels more businesslike. "The scars on your thighs and your legs," he starts, and I look at him, puzzled. I always cover my legs with thigh high stockings and garter belts. "I saw when you were sleeping here the other night," he says, as if reading my mind. "Who did that to you?" he asks. I tell him it doesn't matter unless he's going to help me. He tells me he'll take care of it for me, which is a thought that has crossed my mind since I saw the photos and the guns. I had thought about it, but I knew for myself that in order for this to be done correctly, I had to be the one in the position to take the power back. I shake my head. "It's just one of those things I have to do myself," I tell him. He nods like he understands, and I tell him I need one of his guns. He asks if I know how to use it and I assure him that I do, reminding him that I grew up in this rural state where everybody owns guns. He tells me he wants to be there in case something goes wrong so he can help me take care of it. I agree.

It's been years since I've seen my old home, and it brings back a rush of intense memories when we arrive. Rob can feel my body shaking on the back of his bike. My mother's car isn't there and she shouldn't be back for at least another hour. When she arrives she will find him dead by my hands and my hands alone. The sky is dark enough to where it's doubtful we will be spotted, but Rob parks to the side by the bushes where he has a good view inside through the windows. I can already see my stepfather sitting and watching TV, a man not yet aware of what awaits him. When I come out I will have blood on my hands that I won't wash off for days. When I look down it will be a beautiful reminder as to what has taken place and how sweet vengeance can be. I imagine him begging for mercy. I get off the back of Rob's bike and he nods at me as I knock on the door, gun in hand. I will show him no mercy, just like he showed me none. This is the night that I reclaim my dreams and my past. This is the night when the nightmares stop forever.

How I Met Svetlana

Red
Portland, Oregon

I WOKE UP IN one of the fancy hotels downtown, with only a very vague recollection of eating someone's fancy cheese platter. I was on a couch near an empty plate; curled up uncomfortably on the couch across from me was the anxious little man from my bleary recollections of the night before. I got up carefully, testing for a hangover and fighting a panic attack. I had to find Sveta.

Sveta lay face down on the bed in the other room, not dead but definitely dead to the world. The clock radio by her hand said 9:37- disgustingly early, but even with a cab I'd be pushing my luck to go home, shower, walk my dog and then get back to Eden in time for my shift. Eden. I splashed water on my face and tried to rinse the awful taste out of my mouth. A night of drinking vodka left me with a cloyingly sweet taste in my mouth that felt a lot like my liver rotting. Ugh. I tried not to look freaked out when the anxious man walked in.

"Hi, I heard water," he said. "Um, are you guys leaving?" He looked hopeful.

"Yes," I said, unwilling to commit to anything that would let him know I had no idea who he was. The cheese plate. Sveta had picked him up at Mary's, which meant that I'd been blacked out at Mary's, again, and my reputation and probably my shifts and income were never going to recover.

Betty would relegate me to day and mid-shifts for the rest of my career for my inability to be a graceful, quiet drunk. Fuck it. Had we had sex in a cab last night? Had the cabbie been egging us on? Jesus.

"Look," I said, trying to pull it together. "I think I ate your cheese plate. I'm not really sure how I got here. I'm sorry she took your bed--" he shrugged, like it sucked to have his bed taken over by a beautiful, wasted Russian, but also like he was gratified that a beautiful, wasted Russian had slept in his bed, even if he hadn't been in it at the time- "but, I really have to go. I have to walk my dog and get ready for work. Do you have a pen and paper? Can I leave my friend a note? I can't wake her up."

"Oh, yeah," he said. "Look, I can let her sleep for another hour or two, but I have to check out at 11."

I felt a little guilty about leaving Sveta, the new found love of my life, alone to deal with this, but not very. How had she gotten us here, and why? I shook her a few more times. "Sveta! Sveta!" I got a faint snore in response. "Okay." I took a deep breath. He handed me a pad of paper and pen, both with the fancy hotel logo on them. I took another deep breath. How did you address the love of your life in a note that announced you were leaving her alone in a hotel room with the strange man she picked up the night before?

Sveta,
I had to go walk my dog and go to work. Call me when you wake up! Xoxo Lily

Did that strike the right balance between concerned and carefree? I couldn't tell. I had to go. "Okay." Another deep breath. "Uh, thanks for letting us sleep here, and for the cheese, and, yeah. Have a great day!" I winced at my uncontrollable tendency to lapse into customer service formulas when at a loss for words.

"Yeah. Good luck," he shrugged, and shuffled into the bathroom.

I ran downstairs, ready to return to the more manageable anxieties of dealing with my neurotic dog and trying not to become a homicidal stripper, leaving Sveta and our already epic passion behind with the closing door.

It was an epic passion though, fueled by alcohol, narcissism, and the weird, suffocating psychosis that was the atmosphere of Magic Garden. It started when she came in on my mid-shift while I was onstage. I was a little drunk and having one of those sets- make that days- where I couldn't make a wrong move. Everything was harmonious and satisfactory. I could feel that I was dancing well, I was being adequately admired and, more importantly, adequately tipped.

I was involved in watching myself in the mirror so I didn't notice when she walked in, but I looked up and the hottest woman I'd ever seen was standing where the dancers usually stood at the end of the bar, talking to the bartender and watching me. Her hair dipped over one eye, a dark-haired Lauren Bacall, and she scrutinized me through heavy black frames that made her look like a stern, scholastic pin-up. She was so hot. I wanted her to be talking about me. There was only one customer at the rack, but I put more effort into dancing, pulling out every trick I could think of, making sure she always got my best angles. I worried about getting offstage and having to walk by her to get to the dressing room, but just before my last song ended, she went to the bathroom. I didn't bother going to the dressing room after all, in case she left before I got back up. I counted my ones and adjusted my top and waited for her to come back, or for Julia to finish pouring a drink so that I could grill her.

Julia and the woman arrived back where I was standing at the same time, but Julia spoke first; "Sveta thinks you're banging, Lily. She would do you" Julia had the honour of being the first girl I'd ever fucked, just a few weeks before when we were both high on Vicodin and cocaine; and since she felt responsible for the re-emergence of my lesbian identity, she was invested in helping me explore it. Also, she loved gossip and thought that the guy I was sleeping with was a big douchebag.

I had to think about it for a second. Sveta was so beautiful it made my heart hurt, and I was terrified of being a let-down in bed, which was kind of how I'd ended up in bed with Julia- practise. "It makes perfect!" she insisted, when I told her my jaw was starting to hurt.

I didn't have to think about it for more than a second though. "Great!" I said. "I feel exactly the same about her." We looked at each other. I thought I'd never seen anyone as beautiful in my entire life. She had sharp, high cheekbones, a wide mouth, and dark eyes under hair curled and styled like she was Veronica Lake. She looked Russian, and she was.

This wasn't the first time we met though; the first time we met we couldn't stand each other. I thought Sveta was a bitter, frumpy housewife, and she thought I was a horribly annoying drunk. It was the summer before, when I was busy adoring yet a different stripper, a girl I'd known through that sex worker non-profit, Danzine. All these older alcoholic women somehow loved having me around- I was an unquestioningly admiring baby sister, a youngster whose drug habit made almost everyone else's look totally under control by comparison, and who doesn't love feeling superior?

Elly was a tiny brunette with big dark eyes and the severe bone structure and mouth of Rossetti's Water Willow. She had a menacing glare when she danced that frightened men. Her most loyal customers were energy-sucking bottoms who just wanted to be criticized and Elly was happy to do it, maintaining all the while that she was helping them. Maybe she was.

We met up downtown and immediately she announced "We need some Jager!" so we walked to the liquor store on 5th Ave. and debated getting a medium or a big bottle, eventually settling on medium. I hadn't yet fully discovered Jager's potential; I was still drinking mixed drinks, my favourite being the "Red-Headed Slut," because for obvious reasons it was easy to get customers to buy me endless rounds. The bartenders made the same jokes every time, and with each round it got easier to laugh at them. I was a little dubious about my ability to drink it straight from the bottle while wandering around downtown Portland at 3pm, but if Elly could do it, so could I. But Elly had a bigger plan.

"Okay, now we have to go to Stumptown. We have to get some cups of ice." I blinked at her. "It's too much to drink straight from the bottle, don't you think? We're not winos or anything!"

"Oh, no!" I agreed with her. "Absolutely not. Plus, I don't think I can drink it straight."

"Oh, yes you can!" she snorted. "It's great. I promise. Listen, this one time me and my best friend Bea were drinking Jager, and we had the craziest night! We somehow ended up at Aja's upstairs, you know, the jackshack above The Inferno? We ended up there and I passed out and they had to put me in the shower to wake me up! I had alcohol poisoning!" She paused. "You won't have alcohol poisoning, the point is, it's very easy to drink, so don't worry about it. I'm getting cups and ice now."

When Jager is poured into plastic cups over ice, it bears a remarkable resemblance to iced coffee. And after the first hour or so of choking it down, it became completely bearable. More than that, it tasted great. We spent a blurry four hours wandering around downtown, arguing about books; Jeannie, our evil manager at The Garden of Eden; and the many flaws of the men we were dating. I felt completely blissful, hopeful that in another hour or two Elly might be drunk enough to want to make out- she'd added to this hope considerably when she admitted to having often had drunken lesbian sex with Bea when they lived together- and then she stopped walking.

"Let's call Rita!" she exclaimed. I blinked, mildly heartbroken. This was going so well. Why would we call Rita? If Elly wanted a threesome, I was out. Unlike many, I had absolutely no desire to sleep with Rita, though I did agree with the Eden consensus that "Rita's ass is proof that God loves us and wants us to be happy." I shook my head. So drunk, and in the middle of the day! Rita might have drugs. "Yeah" I said.

Rita, it turned out, was at a porn store only a few blocks away, trolling for new stripper outfits. The selection was not good, but they had some cute shoes. Rita was taller than me, and thus unable to wear the 8-inch heels I favoured when I worked with Jeannie, who preferred that her dancers "look like little ladies" in front of her, despite the fact that the ceiling over the stage was just barely over 6 feet high. At 5' 10" Rita was relegated to 4-inch heels- 5 if she was willing to slouch around for 5 hours. She poked disconsolately at the mammoth heels I was carrying, and then shrugged.

"Let's go back to my place! It's two blocks away. Elly, Sveta is coming over!"

"Sveta!" Elly shrieked. *Great*, I thought. We will never make out. I wonder if it's too late for me to get a hold of Crispin. Crispin was the cabbie I was sleeping with, cabbies being on a similar schedule to strippers and thus easy to get to know and fuck. Elly burbled on. "Lily, she worked with us at Garden of Eden in the old old days! I can't believe she's back! Let's go!"

"Okay," I said, clinging to the hope that someone, somewhere, would have some blow for me. Maybe Sveta.

And Sveta did have drugs. She brought whip-its with her from the Vancouver suburbs, and that was about her only redeeming quality that I could see, because she looked like a glum, plump housewife in an unflattering bulky sweater. I have a quiet but intense love for all things Russian, and I really wanted to like her, but she made it hard. She stared at me meanly through her thick black glasses. "Since when we hang out with cheeldren, Rita?" she drawled in an accent even thicker than her frames. "I have child at home. God I'm sick of them!" She had to have been around the same age as Rita and Elly, 29 to 32, but she seemed ancient.

"Aw, Lily's okay," Rita brushed her off. "Have another whip-it." I cannot do whip-its. I discovered this with Blair, who loved them. Whip-its make me have full-on, nightmarish hallucinations and I hate them, but this situation was already so nightmarish I figured a little nitrous couldn't hurt. "Give me a balloon!" I commanded. I breathed in and fell into a horrible hallucination that an evil dwarf was beating me and causing the end of the world. What felt like a full, apocalyptic eternity later, I slowly raised my head. Rita and Elly were filling more balloons. "No, I'm good, thanks," I said, reaching for the Jager.

I sat on the floor by the couch, drinking and flipping through Rita's pile of magazines. I admired how clean her apartment was. It was spare in an aesthetic way, not simply empty the way mine was. After six months in my current apartment I'd only just obtained a real mattress. I'd been sleeping on an air mattress on the floor, and aside from a couch that smelled like cat pee, donated to me for a nominal fee by my old neighbour, that was it. My books were shelved in milk crates or stacked in carefully ordered piles on the floor of my otherwise empty dining room. Rita had two whole couches and a coffee table. It was astounding to me that people, strippers, lived like this. For the past few years my top financial priorities had been books and blow, and they were about equal in importance. Once during a horrible comedown that had me wandering the streets and crying, I'd cured myself by going to Powell's and spending all my rent money on books. Blair had gotten mad at me about it, because it meant I didn't have any money for anything else (read, blow), but it just meant working a few extra shifts and the club was already basically the center around which my universe spun. Rita clearly didn't share this mindset.

Whatever her habits (and I'd heard they were expensive and debilitating), they didn't affect her home. Her apartment was warm and comfortable, an excellent place to get drunk and do whip-its.

After a while it was decided that Rita, Sveta, and I should go to the supermarket across the street and get food. Elly wanted to take a bath, and Rita's boyfriend couldn't be bothered to move, although he was funding the expedition. By this time I was beyond wasted and once again having fun. Rita pushed our cart through the store like a little old lady, Sveta bossily recommended or nixed food items, and I scouted ahead, desperately craving sushi. When I finally found the little pre-made boxes of it I was captivated, and completely unable to move. Sushi had never looked so delicious. I picked two boxes of each kind, and went off to find my cohorts. Rita and Sveta were not too distant, hunched over the seafood counter and debating the possibilities of lobster. I dropped all my sushi into the cart as they finally decided that yes, they would take the lobster after all. I was appalled. Sushi was one thing, but lobster?

"You aren't paying for that, are you?" I asked, scandalized. "You better be taking that through U-Scan! Lobster!"

Sveta and Rita glared daggers at me. Rita kicked me. "Make her shyut up!" Sveta hissed, but I couldn't. I followed them through the store, helplessly bleating pleas to not pay for the lobster, to "sneak it through the U-Scan!" Sveta wanted to kill me. Rita, who had spent a considerable amount of time in jail and was thus somehow more relaxed about the possible repercussions of a life of crime, kept clucking soothingly at her while giving me warning pinches. Eventually I lapsed into silence, and we made it through the U-Scan unscathed, lobster unpaid for.

Outside Sveta swore. "Holy sheet." She began spouting what I could only assume were swearwords in Russian, hilarious as they sounded to me. "пошел на хуй, blat. My god!" She calmed down and gave me a measuring look through her glasses. "I am going to kill you." I was appalled. This frumpy, evil woman wanted to kill me. I hated her. No matter how much I loved Elly and liked Rita, I was not enduring that bitch's company for one more hour. After the sushi, that was it!

Back at Rita's apartment we set the food up in her tiny kitchen. The lobster got pride of place on a big cookie sheet and they went to town, cracking open its shell and pulling apart its flesh. I'd never seen anything that looked that much like a corpse, but I snuck a piece of lobster meat too, as a consolation prize for being an inebriated idiot and humiliating myself. I squashed myself into a corner and tried to eat my sushi unobtrusively, afraid to bring any more Russian rage down on my head. Sveta ignored me and Rita's boyfriend patted me on the shoulder when no one was within earshot. "You're only young once," he told me. "You'll get older and learn how to hold your liquor and then everyone else will annoy you."

Right, I thought. How comforting. I texted frantically, trying to find some event that would give me a plausible excuse to get away from them before they brought out the nitrous again. "I have to go!" I told everyone around me. "I'm meeting my friend. Bye!" Elly jumped up to hug me and Rita and her boyfriend waved goodbye languorously from the couch. I'm pretty sure I heard Sveta snort. I cringed again, but consoled myself with the thought that such a drab housewife had probably given up dancing for good, and I never had to see her again.

I set off towards the show, determinedly thinking cheerful thoughts about all the ways in which Crispin and I would do it when he got off work at 4 am. As I crossed Burnside I heard a screech of tires and a thump. I'd almost gotten run over by a cab. Behind the wheel I saw Beautiful Noah, my friend Myrna's boyfriend. He was clinging to his steering wheel, with the look of someone who has had a very narrow escape. I stopped walking to wave at him, "Hi Noah!", and heard another screech and some honking. Noah buried his head in his arms and the steering wheel, and I turned around to find that someone else had just barely avoided running me over. The little pedestrian sign had a red hand, and the cars had a green light. I gasped and scampered to the other side of the street, thinking regretfully of poor Noah and the stress I must have just put him through, and the fact that Myrna would probably be hearing about this.

I shook it off and made it to the bar where my friend Seven was. I told him all about Elly and my new drink, Jager, and I forgot about Sveta. I didn't think about her again for months, until she started dancing again, and then only to make sure to never schedule myself with that dour, unpleasant Russian.

And now here she was, standing in front of me, so much more beautiful than I remembered. The glasses were still there, but their severity was sexy rather than bitchy. Sveta seemed similarly unable to connect me with the drunk girl from six months ago. "I deedn't recognize you," she purred. "You were so annoying that day! I would never have thought you look like this. You need a drink. Come sit here."

Immediately we were obsessed with each other. She sat at my rack for the rest of my shift, throwing piles of ones on the stage and encouraging everyone else to do the same. I did flips over the rail to lie on the rack with my head in her lap. She would cover my chest in ones and we would just gaze at each other. Customers who weren't into lesbian tension got bored and left, and even the ones who were felt neglected after the fourth set in a row where I didn't go near anyone but Sveta.

After work it was more of the same. We sat together at the bar, talking nonstop. A lot of it was complete bullshit. Somehow we got onto the subject of Union Jack's and Ilya; Sveta told me solemnly "He has the soul of a poet. I promise. He not always like he is now, fat and stupid." Ilya, the soul of a poet? If it had been anyone else feeding me that ridiculous line I would have laughed in their face, laughed myself sick and then vowed never to talk to anyone that deluded again, but said in a Russian accent it almost made sense. In fact, it sounded insightful and poetic. I nodded.

The customers around us kept trying to lean in and distract us from each other, and Sveta would brush them away with one hand, not looking away from me. It worked with most of them, but one man buzzed around us like a persistent fly. He bought us drinks, and that was good, but then he wanted to talk. Sveta made a face at me. "Why don't you tip Rita?" she asked, and the guy thought that was a good idea. He pulled out his wallet and took some money, and then walked away, leaving his wallet on the bar by us, cash spilling out of it all the way to my elbow. We looked at each other; Sveta's face was mobile and expressive and it was beaming greed and glee. I nodded at her and swept the money into her outstretched purse just before the customer returned. He didn't notice at first, and I could feel Sveta shaking with laughter, but I wanted to get out of there quickly, before he noticed. I stood up. "Well, we should be going," I said.

"Wait, wait!" He hit the counter for emphasis. "Let me buy you ladies another drink before you leave."

"Oh, I don't think--"

"Yes!" said Sveta. "Two blueberry Stolis and cranberry."

Was she crazy? We'd just taken almost all of his money. I only left a few ones in there to stave him off from noticing immediately, until we were gone. I glared at her and she looked back at me, widening her eyes in exaggerated innocence, and if I hadn't been paying attention before, that right there should have told me she was fucking insane. I sat back down and waited for our doom. The drinks came and I pounded mine. I figured even if the extra alcohol didn't add to my suavity it would at least help me brazen it out. The guy, let's call him John, opened his wallet to pay and stared at it. Then looked at us. I felt my eyes widening to as improbable a degree as Sveta's. "Where's my money?" he demanded.

"I don't know," I gasped. "Isn't it in there?" More silent laughter from Sveta's side.

He snarled at me. "No, you know goddamn well it isn't in there!"

I looked helplessly at the bartender, no longer sweet, complicit Julia but Ginny, Jeannie the manager's feeble and wishy-washy daughter. Ginny was only 32 but she looked much older, worn down by being a crackhead with questionable taste in men; by her three children who were continuing the family tradition of being dishonest and untrustworthy; and by living with her tyrannical and terrifying mother. Ginny was stuck in a late 80s fashion vortex: she backcombed her bangs and wore sweaters with odd beaded and satin patterns on the shoulder. On someone else it might have been attractive, but the defeat apparent in her backcombed bangs over-road any potential ironic commentary.

Ginny vacillated between being understanding and easy-going, and being an annoying hard-ass who reported back to her mother if you didn't sell enough drinks or otherwise shirked your stripper duties. The odds of getting out of here unfired were good- both Jeannie and Ginny loved drama, the shadier the better- but Jeannie might put me on Saturday morning shifts indefinitely for upsetting a customer.

I glared at John and tried hard to project an aura of outraged innocence. "Are you joking? That is not funny! Do you know how much money I made today? Why would I steal your money? Not to mention I work here and that would be the stupidest move ever!" I looked back at Ginny, who was nodding, and felt encouraged; she had obviously decided that the bar's honour was being impugned by extension. I felt safe enough to lay it on really thick. "You, sir, are very drunk. You've been here for hours and you've been tipping very well," -Sveta started laughing again at that- "and I think you may have just miscalculated how much money you had."

Ginny nodded. "I think if you're that drunk maybe you should leave," she added. "I'm sorry for over-serving you."

John hit the bar, hard. "I am not that drunk!" he bellowed, which only made him look drunker.

"Leel." Sveta pulled on my hand. "I don't like that man. Let's go."

"I'm sorry you guys," Ginny apologized to us. "Have a good night! Sveta, I'll see you Tuesday."

"Bye Gee-nny!" Sveta trilled, and I wondered how, when mother and daughter were working together, they could tell who she was talking to. Whatever. I waved at Ginny too, and we escaped into the night. Outside the bar Sveta collapsed against the wall, nearly doubled over with the hilarity of it all. I grabbed her and pulled her into a nearby cab, worried about John who would probably be exiting soon after us.

A short time later I blacked out, with only dim recollections of making out in the cab, unzipping her jeans and the cabbie yelling something, in encouragement or outrage I don't remember. We drove around downtown for what seemed like an eternity; it was December and I remember looking at the cab window, at the neon lights reflected in the rain on the glass, and thinking that I had been transported to some amazing lesbian noir, complete with dangerous femme fatale in thrilling deshabille below me. At some point we ended up in Mary's, where Sveta picked up the anxious man and insisted that he take us back to his hotel, but the how or why of all that has remained a mystery. She certainly didn't remember when she called me the next morning.

Cheeques

J.D Angelis
Linden, New Jersey

"So, is this *all* you do?" If only I had a dollar for every time I was asked that question. While most of the clientele was always friendly and respectful, judging by the vibe coming off of him and the tone of his voice, this one clearly was the exception to the rule. "No," I politely replied, not wanting to continue the conversation. Apparently I was the only one. "Lemme guess; you're working your way through school like the rest of the broads here, right?" As thick as my skin is, I felt my blood slowly start to boil. "Actually yes; I do go to school," I replied abruptly. "Yeah right honey. Whatever you say. So tell me, do you suck dick or don't you?" I smiled and leaned in closer over the bar, making sure I had his full attention. I looked him dead in the eye. "Actually honey," I purred, "I do suck dick. I suck GREAT dick. I just don't suck YOUR dick."

I smiled and walked away, knowing it was going to be a very long night. As I made my way down the bar I heard him call after me, "You don't know shit bitch! You're just another stupid stripper. What the fuck do you know?" He wasn't actually asking so I didn't bother replying. The exchange did, however, get me thinking about Socrates; "The only true wisdom is in knowing you know nothing." If I'm just a stupid stripper, what do I know from my years on stage? Have I learned anything? When you've done it for so many years, sometimes all of those nights combined just seem like one really, really long one.

I look around at the clientele. Why are they here tonight? The older gentleman in the corner has a wife with cancer who is undergoing chemo; I know he is here for "safe" female companionship and to forget his fear of losing the love of his life, albeit for just a little while. I know the friendly young guy at the end is a pathological liar. I've listened politely many times to his self-aggrandizing stories without pointing out the logical flaws and inconsistencies, since his stories only lift himself up without ever putting anyone else down. He, too, requires "safe" female companionship. He knows he will never go home with anyone here and doesn't try to; rather, he is practicing to get up the nerve for when he meets the real thing.

What else do I know? I turn to the other side of the bar and reflect on the back country redneck up here in the Northeast on a construction job for a few weeks. After incessantly hounding me an hour ago for my phone number, and me finally giving him one, I know he has a cocktail napkin in his pocket with my stage name and 123-4567 written next to it. "Don't you worry none now honey. Ima call you. Ima make a REAL woman out of you," he tells me through a relatively toothless grin, all the while staring at the meat in my thong between my legs. I know he's going to be really disappointed when he dials that number from his hotel room later. I also know I'll be sorry I won't get to be a fly on the wall and see the look on his face.

I zero in on the heavily buzzed guy in the blue shirt and trucker hat. I know that last week when he was here and I was wearing a slightly sheer shirt, he kept demanding to see my nipples, which is against the law in this state (no nudity where alcohol is sold). "Sorry," I told him, "but I don't have any." He didn't buy it. "Oh BULLSHIT. Now let me see them." I got quiet, looked around, and with a deathly serious expression leaned over the bar and beckoned him toward me, as if to tell him a secret. "Listen, I cover them like this with my hands just like the other girls so no one will think I'm different." I saw he was a little unsure, but definitely intrigued. "What happened?" "I don't really like to talk about. I just want everyone to think I'm like the other girls." I knew I had him on the hook. "You can tell me. I promise I won't tell anyone." "Okay, if you really have to know I lost them two years ago in a freak picnic accident, but I really don't like to talk about it." At that point, I figured he was going to realize I'd been fucking with him. Instead, he picks up a wad of his bills off the bar, looks me right in the eye and with a slightly horrified but sympathetic expression says quietly, "I am so sorry," and stuffs the wad in my hand. I didn't know that was going to happen. I do know my long-time regular customer sitting next to him almost fell off his barstool as beer came out of his nose from laughing. I also know lighting won't strike there twice, so I leave trucker hat alone now.

I turn my attention to my coworkers; what do I know of them? I know the skinny blonde who had worked the day shift was an athletically curvy, young, sweet and bubbly college student when I first met her. I know I warned her not to get caught up in the party atmosphere and to treat this as a business. I know that unfortunately she didn't heed my warning, and now she's gaunt and rail thin from all of the alcohol and coke. I know she claims she's going back to school next semester. I also know she isn't.

I watch Sloane, the incredibly voluptuous, tall, blonde bombshell from Poland bat her beautiful blue eyes at a group of guys she has enraptured. She raises her eyebrows, puts her fingertip to her cheek and pouts her perfect, full lips. I can hear her schoolgirl giggle as one of the guys tells her how he wants to bend her over and fuck her hard. I watch her give an Oscar-worthy performance in the role of blonde bimbo. I know in fifteen more minutes she will be giving me the investment tips she promised, and I know they are wise choices because she's a C.P.A. with a Master's degree in Finance from an Ivy League school. I also know that the money those guys are showering her with will likely be going into her offshore bank account.

A drunk twenty-something woman comes in and decides she wants to audition. It's a little slow, so the manager decides to let her. I take one look at her and immediately know two things: first, she has recently given birth. It's clear that her body has not "bounced back," and she doesn't seem to have been very athletic to begin with. Simply put, she is not "stripper material." Secondly are her facial features; I know by her widely set down-sloping eyes and the wide, flat bridge of her nose that she is the result of Fetal Alcohol Syndrome, and it's likely her newborn looks similar to her. I know the audition will be a disaster. I didn't know she would actually swing herself right off of the pole and stage, slam herself into the cooler, then laugh because she is too drunk to feel it. I know the manager is going to catch hell for letting her on stage to begin with.

As my set ends I retreat to the top bar in the safe shadow of the bouncer, not feeling much like conversing. In a matter of minutes, I quickly survey what I know of my surroundings. The older, burly biker in the corner quietly sips his soda as most of the other girls avoid him because he's "weird." I know he's a Vietnam Veteran still suffering the effects of PTSD. I make a mental note to say hello next set. He's always polite and "weird" never bothered me. Near the break in the bar is the good-looking body builder who thinks he's god's gift to women. I know this is a facade and he's a textbook Narcissist, arrogant on the outside but deeply insecure, and in desperate need of attention and affirmation. In the far corner sits the heavily-published nuclear physicist, whom no one but I and one other dancer knows is a nuclear physicist. I know he cheats on his wife with his mistress, and on his mistress with his girlfriend. I know he tells them all the truth about it; I also know none of them believe him and all think he's joking.

Honesty is the best policy. I decide to sit with him later because I don't judge, and the stories are always hilarious.

I watch the bartenders pick up the pace as the crowd fills in. I have tended bar for years and it's usually my first love and something I really enjoy doing, but I don't envy them tonight. Although I feel like I'm under a microscope when I'm on stage, I know I am in full control of my interactions, as well as the extent of that interaction. If I don't want to say a word to anyone, I don't have to. When you tend bar, you are stuck with whomever sits in your section, whether you want them there or not. It's the bartender's job to keep the party moving forward, but not let it fall off the cliff. I see John walk in and sit down to a pint that the bartender already has waiting for him. He waves and I wave back, thinking of the night he was going through a rough patch, I was serving him and had to cut him off. I put a pint of club soda in front of him instead of beer and explained that what he drank an hour ago hadn't even hit him yet. If he kept going at that pace his night would end quickly, and I wanted him to get home in one piece. He drank club soda the rest of the night and always tips me very well whether bartending or stripping. We both know I saved him from himself that night.

I see Tony and his friends arrive; all are regulars. Tony is usually pretty cool and funny, until one night he had a few too many and thought it would be cute to reach over the bar and smack me on the ass. I put him in a wrist lock, spun around and told him in no uncertain terms that if he did it again I would punch him in the face. Fair warning. Of course excessive alcohol and being a smartass don't mix. His jaw was sore for two days. I know I have a mean left hook, and now he does too. He apologized and hasn't stepped over the line since.

Chris and her fellow construction worker buddies arrive. She nods to me and heads for the pool table. She's very butch and lesbianism is not yet quite mainstream, so she always hangs back from the bar and focuses on her game of nine ball. I flash back to the first night she tipped me. With a few beers in her she came up to the bar, called me over, tipped me and said, "Damn- too bad you're engaged." She's been my protector ever since and looks out for me whenever she's there. One night a guy was getting a little out of hand with his hands and although I'm always sober and usually pretty quick, before I could even react she had his arm up behind his back and was asking me if his face needed to meet the door on the way out. I told her it was cool. Since then I know she has my back.

As the night winds down and I prepare for my final set, I sit in the dressing room looking into myself in the mirror. What have I learned about myself? What do I know about the image staring back at me? I know that in this moment I'm going to put on my favorite black tango dress with the slit up the side, my long black gloves and my oversized black hat and request Santana's Black Magic Woman. I know I'm going to block out the crowd for that song, and just let the music move through me, feeling the need to express myself creatively, physically painting a moving picture of fluid motion and sensual lines. I know that I can actually dance, and right now I want to dance just for me. And not that it matters at that moment, but I know there are those in the crowd who will "get it" on the artistic level and appreciate it.

But what have I learned from all of those long nights rolled into one? I've learned that I can size people up within the first three minutes, and if I trust my instinct it is never wrong, even knowing someone for years thereafter. The men are definitely not alike, and neither are all women. I've learned that I can stare a guy down and give him a hard-on, while mentally making a grocery list. I've learned that there is nothing wrong with recognizing and celebrating my sexuality. Most importantly, I've learned that other people's opinions of me do not dictate who I am. I've learned that stripping is an art, a great outlet for physical visual expression, and even fun, but should be treated as what it is-- a business. If you do that, it can take you places. It took me into a Ph.D. program having just a Bachelor's degree, but what the fuck do I know? I'm just another stupid stripper.

From Elation to Emptiness

Orchid Souris Rouge
Portland, Oregon

I LOVE THE ATMOSPHERE of the club almost as much as I love performing naked in front of a crowd of enthusiastic onlookers. It's a spectacle one can only find at The Kit Kat Club, unless of course you have a time machine and decide to take it back to the eras of cabarets and dance halls. Glasses clink, slam down on tables and occasionally shatter on the floor. Patrons and dancers are laughing and flirting. The crisp cash crinkles as it's pulled from wallets, folded into origami and passed from patron to dancer or laid to rest on the rack. Other times the bills click furiously onto the wooden stage floor as they make their descent. Behind delicate, sheer, red curtains the bodies of dancers twist, arc and undulate in a particularly sensual fashion, each body in its own stage of undress. The eyes of the patrons glaze over as they lose themselves to these deceptively private moments with the beautiful creature of their choosing.

As I make my way to the dressing room I pass the stage. The dancer occupying it is collecting her tips from a very decorative seated position. A laugh escapes her red lips as she winks at a patron. I smile to myself at having witnessed this moment. It felt like sweetness coated in raw sexuality. Realizing I had ceased my steps to watch, I returned my attention to the thick red velvet curtain in front of me. My hand slides between the curtains, revealing my wrist like a Geisha to the girls on the other side. Two dancers sit in front of the mirror, both intently staring into their own eyes as they touch up their lashes and lips. As they each find their satisfaction with the face in the mirror they fall into conversation.

Walking into the rear portion of the dressing room I am confronted by bags overflowing with all manner of clothing, costuming and lacy lingerie. I greet one of my favorite dancers who is seated next to my things. Her pale skin has been dusted lightly with shimmering powder and she smells like citrus and sex. I blush at the thought of it and then realize she's looking directly at me. Her right eyebrow raises slightly as she grins devilishly which only serves to make the blush on my cheeks deepen. I smile back as confidently as I can manage to before I turn my attention to changing my costume. Reaching blindly into a bag my hand finds the lapis blue, satin skirt and matching bra. There's something to be said for wearing and performing in a costume you made yourself. The skirt is long in the front and shamelessly short in the front, almost resembling a burlesque style bustle skirt. The fabric is adorned with hollow, etched, silver beads.

Once dressed I change into my tallest stilettos, 8 inches of glorious, man-made fantasy, the underneath of which laces up like a corset. The timing is perfect; as I look myself over once more in the mirror I hear my name being called over the microphone. I live for this. I make my way back through the curtains of the dressing room and up the stairs to the stage. I hear a few people remark on the absurdity of my shoes, "How can she even walk in those," they remark. I feel like an evil genius as I look one patron in the eyes and tell them slyly, "Just wait until you see me defy gravity in them." Inhale, exhale, I smile from ear to ear as the first song starts. I grasp the brass firmly and lift myself with a deliberate slowness, the momentum from my movements causing the pole to spin. My hair brushes across my face giving me brief glimpses of more and more people taking seats to watch my performance. My body rises, descends and orbits in mid air, occasionally coming down to crawl my way across the stage floor. I brush my cheek gently, like a harmless little kitten, against the arm of a patron. He smiles and I can see a spark of titillation behind it.

As my performance comes to a close I find myself feel completely elated, nude and glistening with sweat. The patrons at the rack, and even a fair amount of those seated farther away at tables, erupt into applause and cheers. There is no greater feeling in this world as a performer than when the audience before you has been touched by the visual feast you've lain before them. I thank each person at the stage for tipping and being lovely, which is extremely important to me. I never want to someone who sees me perform to feel hollow afterwards because I failed to connect with them. I want people to walk away feeling as though they had stumbled into a beautiful, hidden world. Unlike the stories of faeryland however, this world can be stumbled across at any time by anybody. It is here for and at the leisure of those who purposefully, or accidentally, find their way through our doors.

Making my way down the stage stairs I see someone approaching out of the corner of my eye. I turn and see the man whose arm I had rubbed against from the stage standing before me with a cocktail in one hand and money in the other. Condensation drips from his glass, his hazy eyes searched mine for a brief moment. I smile flirtatiously at him as he asks if I'm available for a private dance. I channel my inner Mae West, "Of course handsome, follow me". And I mean it, this man is particularly handsome. He's tall and looks to be in decent shape, his dark hair is short and well groomed, his face is clean shaven and smooth. He has on brand new jeans, black leather motorcycle boots and a plain black long sleeved shirt. In the darkness I cannot tell what color his eyes are but they seem warm and maybe even the slightest bit inviting. Passing by him so that I may lead us to our destination, I inhale traces of his cologne and my nipples harden.

Work doesn't have to always be arduous and I'm delighted to dance for someone well kempt and attractive. All of the booths have been vacated but the perfumes of the other dancers still linger in the dim light. A feeling of unease begins to weave its way outwardly from my core when my patron temporarily refuses to have a seat. I watch him stagger momentarily before he finally relents and sits down. "Let me take your drink for you" I say gently, "I'd hate for it to get spilled." All manner of respect is draining from this drunken man, I can see him entertaining desires that I will not be satisfying with what I'm willing to offer. That's when I notice the wedding band on his finger. I start to wonder what his relationship with his wife must be like. I doubt it's a happy one. I can only hope they have no offspring to speak of for if they do- I decide not to let my mind take that thought further.

"Are you going to dance or not?" He asks. The aggression in his voice is not surprising, considering the amount of alcohol he must have consumed by now, but it is no less off-putting. I make my voice as honey sweet as possible, "Of course I am. I was simply going to wait for the next song. I'd be happy to start now if you like." When he fails to respond I start my dance. It's all a routine at this point. I don't have anything to give other than an illusion because he's not even paying attention to my dance as much as he's contemplating how to touch me without being caught or reprimanded. This well dressed monster is no longer able to hide beneath the veneer of his appearance. He's just another slimeball dressed in gentleman's clothing.

Turning and swaying as seductively as I can manage under duress, everything is reduced to slow motion the moment I notice his hand moving towards my right breast. Despite my noticing, his fingertips manage to brush against my flesh before I can push them away. The feeling of an aggressive, unwelcome touch sets my blood and body aflame. "There's no touching allowed, and you don't strike me as the type of man who's never been to a strip club before. If it happens again I'm more than happy to introduce you to our bouncer," I say angrily. I only catch half of his poor attempt to make an excuse for such absolutely inappropriate behavior, because I know he's going to try again. I feel so violated and disrespected that the feeling of excitement as his being kicked out overrides my better judgment. "Go ahead and do it again" I think to myself.

And he does. However, this time he's much bolder, almost as if my reprimand spurred him on. In an attempt to keep my distance he manages in his drunken state to lean forward and lick my left shoulder blade. Because I refuse to be mistreated and go unpaid, I grab his wallet which he had chosen to remove from his pocket and place on the shelf behind us. He fails to notice until I hastily put my ballet flats on and run, wallet in hand, to our bouncer who promptly follows me back to the private dance area. The patron is so saturated in alcohol that he hasn't moved from the cushioned leather seat. The bouncer opens the wallet I handed to him, takes out what I'm owed and grabs the man by his arm. "Sir, it's time for you to leave now." What is about to unfold is something I never want to be involved in. I take my money, gather my clothes and make my exit as confrontation ensues.

The night is coming to a close and all I can think to do is retreat to the dressing room. Several deep breaths and half a cocktail later I approach the DJ booth. The DJ and I chat for a few minutes before he lets me know that I won't be going onstage again. I thank him more genuinely than he probably realizes. Once again I find myself in the dressing room, my sanctuary from the chaos. A few spots previously occupied by other dancers have long since been cleared off and packed away into lockers and garment bags. There exists no trace of confidence; I no longer feel sexy or beautiful. Quite the opposite. I feel violated and hollow. Letting my muscle memory take over, I put each item in its proper place. Money is counted out so that tips can be dispersed accordingly to the bartender and DJ. Bags in hand, I approach the bouncer, hand him a fistful of angrily wadded bills and ask if he could please walk me out to my car. I've had quite enough at this point and I know he can sense it. He looks at me sympathetically as I hand over my heaviest bag, my feet already leading me towards the exit.

I go from the club, to my car and finally through my front door. My lover is already there awaiting my return, but the excitement I had previously felt at the thought of peeling off every stitch of clothing on my body in front of his groggily excited gaze has been replaced with a feeling of disgust and degradation. All I want to do is shower and wash off the touch of an ungrateful, misogynistic, sorry excuse for a human being before making my way to bed and hopefully to dreamless sleep. It's never been easy to remain calm and diplomatic in the face of sexual assault. Even more difficult is mastering the task of forcing oneself to let go of what happened, such that one can continue making their living in the sex industry.

"How was work?" the scantily clad man in my bed asks as he rubs one hand over his closely cut blonde hair. "It was alright until I gave a last minute dance to a groping piece of shit." I say as I hastily remove my clothes and crawl into bed. While I didn't intend for my words to come out so bitterly, it happens anyway. I feel his strong arms wrap around me gently, the muscles beneath his smooth flesh flex, harden and then relax. "I'm so sorry princess." His beautiful blue eyes search mine but I look away because the tears are starting to form. Unable to respond, our conversation ends, but I feel so very grateful for his love and tenderness- for it is exactly what I need.

I turn my focus to his large, well sculpted hands which have found their places, one on my recently violated breast and the other on my ribs. His touch soothes me; it erases the unwelcomed contact from an hour ago. I study the tattoos on his arms, and focus on their bright colors and intricate designs: a portrait of Medusa on one forearm and a portrait of a satyr girl on the other. Oak leaves and playing cards make up the backgrounds of each sleeve. I am reminded of the depth of his spirit. I become lost in the recollection of little moments we've shared. Feeling his warm breath and soft lips on the back of my neck, serenity is mine once again.

Despite being comforted I lay awake as my brain tries to wrap around what happened. How can anyone come to the conclusion that it's perfectly acceptable behavior to touch a stranger in a sexual manner, or any other manner for that matter, without first asking for their permission? Especially in a strip club. Much like the items in a museum or the images on a movie screen, I'm not meant to be handled in any way whatsoever. My obligation as a dancer is to be a beautiful, moving work of art and a source of sexual excitement but from a distance. Are lap dances intimate in nature? Absolutely. Are they meant to pave the way to heavy petting, or even the even more nausea inducing fluid exchange? Absolutely not. How would the man I wanted to tear to pieces feel if he had a daughter and she was treated the way he treated me? My eyelids feel like lead, exhaustion begins to consume me. I manage to whisper good night to which my love responds by pressing his lips tenderly against my neck once more.

Tomorrow is another day.

Haikus, An Intermission

A bill on the stage
I peer closer, hopeful, yet
It's a goddamn one.

High heels are like cocks:
Tall and thick are impressive
But scare me to death

If you kiss my neck
While I'm giving you a dance
We will not be friends.

Customer thinks that
My pussy is wet, aroused
Nope. Leaking tampon.

Customer in suit:
My heart leaps, until he
Orders PBR.

I think I'm in love
With the man on the hundreds
Mr. George, I'm yours.

The ugly stripper
Has a better ass than me
Let's piss in her purse

The DJ is drunk
Fleet Foxes will surely be
The death of us all.

Regular comes in
Whines about his wife and job
God Bless the yuppies

A Sixty-Something Persian Guy Peed On Me and All I Got Was $20

Kat Montana

BEING TOLD BY a strip club DJ that he thinks about you when he works out is only slightly preferable to hearing that you're getting heavy rotation in the spank bank, climbing two spots since last week. I was able to go about my life ignoring the fact that someone was out there grunting while an image of me hovered over a bench press, until I was confronted with a gym self-portrait in my inbox. It was when I found myself having to dance to "She Hates Me" by Puddle of Mudd on a regular basis that I decided to find a new club.

I went to Cabaret in downtown Portland and wish I had been sexually harassed sooner, because it was a fucking blast right up until it was shut down and turned into a seafood restaurant. It was in the final week of Cabaret's existence that I had an all-time first in my stripping career: a customer urinated on me. The manager missed it because he was in the hospital with a "brown recluse bite," that was most definitely actually an abscess. His Men's Warehouse suit was crumpled and he looked like he hadn't slept all night before coming straight to the club from the ER. When I told him that a guy peed on me during a dance, he stopped writing with the hand that wasn't in a sling. "He like, whipped his *dick* out and shit?!" He waited, slack-jawed with shock and anticipation, but also in a lots-of-painkillers kind of way. I had to clarify that no, the creep did it from inside his pants. "So he didn't really pee on you. He just wet his pants." I could tell that he was disappointed, even in his medicated state. He wasn't grasping the severity of the situation. I made the case that the perp intentionally wet his pants on (under) me.

I hadn't realized that anything out of the ordinary was happening until I stood up and the air hit the man's urine, giving me a wet sensation and letting me know that the whole back and inside of my upper thigh was covered in something. An inventory of what fluids the body produces flashed before me. Immediately I thought that it was blood or some other kind of vaginal fluid because I was about to start my period. He was wearing black pants and I couldn't see much of anything in the dark. I felt it and examined the residue on my fingers. There was too much of it and it seemed too thin, too clear. My embarrassment turned to suspicion and I decided it came from his body and not mine. Could it be semen? But again, it was so watery and there was so much of it. I knew that the only way I would start getting some answers was if I raised my hand to my nose.

It was an unmistakable, unquestionable smell. It's something that cannot be synthesized; it was a city street, it was missed urinals. It was piss so foul that it can only excreted by the human male. "Um, your pants are wet." I felt like I was bluffing.

"Oh, it's okay. I spilled a beer earlier. It's okay." Something about the way that he was reassuring me felt wrong.

"I think this dance is over." I left him on the couch as I ran off in search of running water, first to the bathroom upstairs that only had one-ply toilet paper that melted when it touched water, and then to the bathroom in the basement where I found a roll of paper towels. I was mad that I was being forced to look over the incontinent. These old guys really need to get their priorities in order.

I was in a state of denial when I opened the door at the top of the stairs to find two girls talking and pointing at the couch. There was a circular wet spot with a sizable diameter. Staring into the spot, I suddenly knew that he did it on purpose. I announced that yes- that was what they thought it was, which was something I was sure of because I had given the guy whom it came out of a dance, and made a point of smelling it. They stared at me with pity and shock and then I could hear them wondering if I still had pee on me. I wanted to assure them that it was totally cool because I took a sponge bath. I felt embarrassed for claiming credit, as if this was part of my usual hustle.

Where was he?? I was filled with rage and paced around the club, looking everywhere, but he was long gone. I vented to the pregnant cocktail waitress about it, I guess because she was the next person I saw, she had always seemed sympathetic to other strippers' plights, and always got me water. I showed her the spot as evidence and she said that she would get the cook to clean it. "You could take a shower," she volunteered. Why hadn't I thought of that?

Maybe it was because I was scared of the shower. It reminded me of a horror movie because it was usually covered in flies and only missing a severed pig's head. I didn't think that it was even functional (It was missing a door!) until I stopped by the club one time during the day in order to get something from my locker. A girl walked into the dressing room in a towel, looking like she got out of a shower. *That's kinda weird*, I thought. Then another girl in a towel grabbed a razor and some bath products and walked in the direction of the bathroom. *Holy shit, the day girls actually use that shower??*

The cook was headed towards the couch when I intercepted him by hysterically trying to yell over the music about towels while making wiping signals. I just assumed that he had been informed that I was the victim of this heinous crime. He apologized that there weren't that many bar rags and that he couldn't help me.

I had only interacted with him once before when I was forced to order bar food one Sunday night because all the places to eat downtown were closed. He cooked me a sad grilled cheese that was black on one side and soggy and uncooked on the other. He faced the charcoaled side down and I was mad that I tipped him before I got a closer look at the mess he tried to pass off as a sandwich. I blurted out that I was the one who had been peed on and needed towels or bar rags because I had to take a shower. "Oh God, that was you? Yeah sure, I'll get you some bar rags. Where is it, anyway?"

There was a man leaned back on the couch centered over the spot, concealing it completely with his body. The tweaker girl was taking her shoes off in preparation to give him a dance. She was wearing a furry vest and a beanie. Earlier in the night, I found myself staring at her and pondering how we were in the same room but dressed for totally different climates. I wasn't sure if meth was actually her drug of choice, but she had the aesthetic of an extra on *Breaking Bad*. One time the manager locked himself out of his office and had to convince her to squeeze through a gap between the dressing room and office wall. The cook discreetly motioned her over, so as not to alert the patron that he was lounging in another man's urine.

"I GUESS YOU HAVE TO MOVE BECAUSE SOMEBODY PEED RIGHT THERE AND HE NEEDS TO CLEAN IT." Apparently she thought honesty was policy in this situation.

My name was blaring overhead. "Kat on the main stage. That's right, here's the sexy Kat, making her way to the staaaage!" The cook promised me he would leave some bar rags on the back of the toilet in the bathroom for me. I felt like hugging him. I did my stage set, trying my best to be sexy while also not touching any part of my contaminated body to any other part of my body.

En route to the shower, I passed the tweaker girl dancing for her customer. No one else was back there. They had their pick of all the best private dance area real estate, yet still decided to go with the stranger's pee. Not only had the revelation that he was sitting in a puddle of piss not deterred the guy from getting dances, but he also decided that a strip club cook wiping down the area was good enough for him. There's no way it could even be dry yet. All that could have happened was some cleaning solution was added and rubbed around as a symbolic gesture. The guy looked delighted to be soaking up the company of a crazy-looking stripper in a beanie and also some dude's byproducts. *Shows what I know.* None of my customers like me that much.

I actually didn't see any flies when I took my long, hot, hand soap shower. I felt like a new woman, and was giving myself a mental pep talk as I touched up my makeup. I was going to salvage what was left of one of my last nights and not let that mean pervert win. A friend came in the dressing room and I told her what happened.

"Which guy was it?!" I told her that he was wearing a striped shirt, short, bald, sixties, and had a beer belly.

"Was he really round?"

"Yes!"

"Was he Persian?"

I had completely forgotten that he had an accent. "Yes!"

"Ali did that?!"

"Do you know him?!"

"No! I just met him tonight but I'm really good with names." That's right, everyone had tried him. He *looked* like he would spend money. I watched every stripper in the room approach him and get turned away. I only asked him for a dance because I was trying not to be lazy, not because I thought he would say yes.

Wait a minute- I was the one that he chose to pee on? Did he see me across the room and say to himself, "That's the one!" What do I look like? And why had I forgotten about his accent? The only time we talked, his rotten breath had caused me to start gagging. I turned my back to him and sat in his lap, gasping for fresh air so that I could regain control of my body. It must have been at the exact same time that he was emptying his bladder.

Jersey Girl

Felicity Hazel
New Brunswick, New Jersey

I STARED DANCING FOURTEEN years ago, and I've danced under more names than I can remember: Angel, Jersey, Sadie, Felicity. I started at a club in, New Jersey, which no longer exists. I can't tell you the name of it anyway, because the owners were mafia, and I ain't trying to make my life harder, you know? Anyway, there was a stage in the center of the bar with two poles on it, and the bartender walked between the bar and the stage. One of the poles went all the way up the ceiling and into the dressing room, so if you happened to be late to stage, you could just slide down it that way. We had anywhere from five to twenty girls on the night shift. I started there a week before my eighteenth birthday. I'd been arrested for selling ecstasy; I was the driver for the salesman. I begged and begged my friend who managed the place to lend me the money, or to get me a job so that I could come up with the money for a lawyer. He fought me tooth and nail too not start dancing. When I started working there I couldn't even walk in heels; I was stumbling, I couldn't dance, I had no rhythm. Now I can run in eight inches, but then? I couldn't do it in little tiny platforms. Two girls took me under their wings and showed me a few moves. They made me walk in the dressing room, but the first time on stage I flew headfirst into the pole. And, then they made me slide down the pole and onto the stage. In two weeks I was good enough to walk across the stage. There was one girl who didn't like me; every time I would try to cross the stage she would purposely do pole tricks, and one night she kicked me so hard it knocked me out. Different from clubs with actual stage performing, you didn't always pick your music.

And nobody does much for pole tricks. In New Jersey it is illegal to tip money at the stages in the girls are topless or nude, and alcohol is served. You do ten to twenty minutes on stage half hour set, depending on how many or few girls there are. After you leave the stage, you walk around, strike up a conversation, and try to get a guy to stick a dollar on your body. Each girl is different; it depends on their morals or whatever. It depends on how badly they need that dollar. A lot of the girls I've seen are heroin addicts, or coke addicts. There are really bad dancers, and to find a club that isn't promoting or allowing drug use is really difficult. One night a girl snuck into the dressing room (where she wasn't supposed to be, since she was a patron at the time), and found her way through a cubbyhole into the attic. Apparently she was looking for a place to shoot heroin. While she was climbing a loose area in the ceiling collapsed, and she fell through the ceiling and onto the stage. She hit her head really badly and the club's response. Most of the girls were told to do private parties, but since I was a friend of the manager I didn't have to, and I stayed out of trouble. For the most part. After several months, the club was about to close its doors; the building was bought out by a big home improvement store chain. I needed a lot of money because I was preparing to move to Los Angeles, and money had been slimmer and slimmer. One night an older guy came in who was tipping in big bills. He was a big guy (not heavy but big), and one of the only customers. My friend and I were paying attention to him since he was paying us; he kept name-dropping, mentioning other strippers he knew, and telling me that I was beautiful. His name was Robert. When the place was closing down for the night, he asked what other plans I had after the place closed. I told him I was trying to save up a lot of money because I was moving to California soon. He asked if I wanted to pick a girl to come home with, saying, "You don't have to do anything to me, but you two can mess around. I'll give you $5,000 each." So I thought about it, and asked,

"We don't touch you, right?" He insisted, no no no. So I asked Michelle, a girl I liked, and then I asked management about it. They said, "He's a good customer, he'd never touched any of the girls. You can leave early if you want." So we had someone's boyfriend act as a bouncer and follow us to Robert's He had photos of his grown children all over the house, both sons and daughters, all older than me. He was divorced. I don't know what he did for a living, but we were in his condos. He had money. It went smoothly; we made out, we got paid. The only problem was he wrote us checks. It wasn't cash, but he hadn't promised cash, so no big deal. We ended up getting his number, and we went back three times. The third time we went, we were hugging and kissing each other when we left, only because we were happy to be alive. The third time wasn't so nice. He got extremely violent with us. His hands were suddenly around our necks, choking with all of his strength, like he was trying to kill us. I was praying and fighting to live, especially since we hadn't had any bouncers follow us. We'd been drinking that night- I had been drinking my usual whiskey- but there were no drugs involved.

It started when Michelle went to shower. I was standing there and he came up to me, put his hands on my neck, and asked me if I ever wanted to see my family again. Of course I started crying like a little girl and trying to fight. Michelle heard me, choking and punching and kicking the wall, and she came running out of the bathroom, jumped on his back and started hitting him, but he just threw her off and went after us both.

As suddenly as it started, he stopped. He stopped, saying that he wanted to see how far he could go. He actually said that. Our necks and faces were red. We were astounded. He wrote me a check for $10,000; I think he gave her a little less. He asked when he could see us again. It was ridiculous, and of course we couldn't go to the police. I would have been arrested for prostitution. After handing us the checks, he told us that if we came back a fourth time, we had to fuck him. We politely declined. And yeah, the checks cleared. I moved to California a couple of weeks later. I remember that he smelled like armpits. The third night, before he attacked us, was different- he sat in the corner, jerking off his huge, thick, ugly penis. The first time he sat and did nothing. The second time he immediately retreated to the bathroom, I think to jack off. So there I didn't worry about him finding my information through the cashed checks, since I knew that I was moving soon. I don't know if Michelle knew enough about banking, or if he could see the full name that cashed the checks. Perhaps if he did this regularly he didn't bother looking. And, back then it was harder to find people. That was before Facebook. Besides her, nobody has ever heard this story; I never told anyone.

I got a couple phone calls from him after I'd moved to California- something like, "come over here and have fun." No thank you. I don't know what happened to the other girl. I don't know a real last name to look her up. She wasn't a girlfriend or lover- we were just working. I sometimes wonder if she's still alive. Michelle is a common first name, I wonder if she's working, found a career. She was 18 or 19 and had just started dancing at that time. She was kind of the nerdy type; she loved science. All of my friends were horror fans, loved Jack Daniel's and metal music. She didn't even drink. I have no idea if I would have made it out alive without her. She came to defend me, she didn't hide. I could have been raped and murdered in that bed, in that room, with all those pictures of his children smiling at me. Sometimes I feel bad for dragging her in to that situation. But she saved me.

I worry about girls who are prostitutes. It makes me wonder what they have to deal with.

I've considered going to work at the Bunny Ranch, but I think once I got there I'd freak out. Memories of that situation might hit me, even in controlled environment. I've been offered stuff like that, and I've always turned them down. Would I ever do that kind of thing again? Fuck no. After that, I'm hesitant to whom I'll give my phone number to. Of course not all people in clubs are bad. I've met some of the closest women friends there. And male friends, like Cowboy Mike? I met him fourteen years ago in a strip club; he was a customer. We'd talk about travel and wanderlust. Over a decade later and he looks out for me like a big brother. He's met every boyfriend I've had since 1999. He would tip me to dance and we'd have conversations. He went to my wedding a couple years ago. Nobody ever thinks about stuff like that. But it happens, and it's good. It's not all bad or evil.

Darlin'

Clementine Oregon

Most hours I'm just passing- waiting for that one opportune moment- the mythical lapse in which something finally gives and I find my mind, my body, my heart- all in agreement with the preponderance that now is the moment when the most viable option is simply to let go. In most narratives, this might be when the writer would let the audience in on their little secret- saying *Oh, but it wasn't always this way. Let me tell you how it happened...* But the truth is it has always been this way. When your childhood bedtime stories consist of a weeping mother recounting the day her daddy walked out of the bathroom frothing at the mouth after sticking a needle full of enough barbiturates to sedate a room full of psychotics into his arm, mere moments after sitting her on his knee and playing a duet of Heart and Soul on the decaying and out of tune upright. When that same woman threatens to leave you to fend for your three, four, five year old self- because you didn't love her enough to clean your room or you asked for something in the store, suicide becomes the embroidered throw pillow, the family dog, the security blanket. It has always been this way. Chances are, at any given moment I've been pondering new methods- like a researcher high on theory; those moments when I'm staring wistfully out the window...I'm devising the perfect formula.

The man to my right at the bar had been patiently awaiting my answer to his question- one I had heard again and again in just six short months; "Why did you start dancing?" His eyes trailed over my bare thighs and ass, landed on the sheer blue of my lace bralette where my nipple was visibly contorted- if Picasso had spent his Blue Period in strip clubs, these are the images he would have painted. He was fulfilling a fantasy, imagining slipping his cock in between my thighs, snaking his tongue over my rosebud areola. He saw my creamy white legs splayed out on a hotel bed; I visualized a silver blade on the edge of a bathtub, a night spent under the stars with a bottle of cheap gin and six months worth of valium, the look on the face of a veteran paramedic when he can't find the pulse on the soft wrist of a twenty-something. I cocked my head to the side and poised myself- coy, another second for posterity…"I decided I'd prefer to regret doing something rather than spend my life wondering what it might have been like, and I actually really love it." I smiled.

The man spun a lone ice-cube in his scotch and casually freed the two top buttons on his collar. "Well, that's good. What did you say your name was again?" I raised an eyebrow inquisitively- "Your name is Michael! And you don't remember mine? Tsk-tsk. It's Clementine." Before he could start in on his personal rendition of "Oh, My Darlin'" my name boomed over the speaker "Welcome to Lucky Devil Lounge ladies and gentlemen, up next we have the lovely Clementine on stage for you!" I stood slowly and pivoted on my toe as I turned to walk to the stage.

It was true. I did love dancing, and when the end of your life could happen at any moment, when you have a disease that hijacks your cognitions and makes death feel as cozy as a hot mug of tea- well, you learn to take things as they come and to live when you can, to take any opportunity that may present some memory, some experience, some relief from the incessant whispers that send chills through your bones as you walk down the street. I stepped onto the stage and grinned at the three men sitting at the rack. The music started- not your typical stripper song, but that's why this was the club I worked at. Moreover, this is why I worked in Portland. There is no such thing as a typical stripper here and I relished that. My flats were coming apart at the seams, the tip of my toenail was visible through the threadbare black cotton. All of those nights I spent dancing in my room as a kid, it was exactly like this. An escape, one of the few times when the hurt dissipated, when my mind was allowed a foray into a world I would never know. I pointed my toes as I traveled across the metal rack, I felt the arch spread from the soles of my feet, up my calf, into my spine- I felt musculature bend and pull beneath my skin, smooth like oil, the heat rose in my body and blossomed out through my mouth, settled deep in my gut and I felt my solar-plexus expand with true breath. For the first time in days, I was whole- no longer in a battle with my nervous system, everything was flowing and humanity was again a place with which I could identify. And for the next seven and a half minutes, I was free.

I closed my eyes, the red light flickering under my lids as I snaked by body around the pole, my feet left the ground, I rose on air- seemingly abandoning the rules of gravity, leaving behind the years and years of weight that I had grown accustomed to hauling around, that perhaps, was the reason why I took such small steps, stayed so quiet, felt so small. But, not here. Here, I was full, grown, sensual, the one place where I found safety in womanhood, a loophole within a society that has taught women to fear their power, to never bare their teeth, let alone their breasts. I often closed my eyes while on stage, the customers, the club, the world, melting away, becoming enmeshed with a sound wave, a vibration, a light beam. The music, that penetrating red glow, my body, and wherever it was my mind had wandered to. "You thinking 'bout fucking the dudes that watch you get naked, aren't ya?" I blinked and turned toward the voice- an older man, dirty fingernails, a baseball cap with a bent rim. He smelled acrid, like rolled cigarettes and cheap vodka. I've never trusted men who drink cheap vodka; it's too easy, there's no thought in it, and I'd found that a man was often well-reflected in his drink. I laughed and sidled my panties half-way down. I'd offer my ass over my eyes any night. Eye contact is something earned, and it takes more than a crumpled dollar bill.

The man let out a satisfied grunt and my mind flowed backward into a memory. A lover stood in the rain, head bent, a long-stemmed red rose dangled at his side. The neon from the theatre lights reflected in the puddles, uncertainty reflected in our eyes. Electricity ran between us even from twenty feet away. My hands were on fire, pressed hard against the pole. Gillian

Welch's words trembled through the speakers; *"My first lover..."* No, I hadn't been thinking about 'Fucking the dudes that watch me get naked'. I had been thinking about the first time I made love, the first time I found myself feeling inexplicably wine drunk, while my glass held only water..."*Quick silver girl and she's free..."* I pulled my now completely nude body up from the stage floor and gathered my lace panties and a handful of crumpled bills. I felt a little shattered. My mind was still in that boy's bedroom with the musical hands, my heart still in his lovely, sharp teeth. I stood, completely nude in front of strangers. I worried, not that they had seen my flushed labia and naked breasts, but had any of them seen even a flicker of emotion cross my face? At that very moment, I wouldn't have been surprised to find warm, sticky-sweet blood on my fingers when I pressed them between my ribs. I wondered if they could see it too. Man #1 leaned back in his chair and happily scratched his groin, #2 counted his money with furrowed brow, and #3 looked into his beer as if his entire future might be held in the dull, yellow foam. Some nights you could be dying in front of thirty men and they'd never even blink.

My chin held high as I walked off stage, I pulled the sheer curtain of the dimly lit private dance room back and let my full weight collapse onto the vinyl bench in a graceless sprawl. I arched my back and stretched, cracked my toes against the floor, rubbed the purple and red bruise that sprawled along the inside of my thigh like spilled paint. I pulled my panties on and held my knees to my chest, smiled and drew a finger over the velvet fleur de lis as I gave one last moment to that lost lover. God, it was a disaster- but it was a perfect disaster and I wouldn't take one second of it back. Not everyone can revisit something so raw and come away from it with a mouth full of nostalgia, sweet and thick like honey.

Out on the patio, the fireplace flickered. A languorous orange tongue licked the air. Hoisting myself onto the red glittered bar stool I crossed my tired legs at the ankles and brought a cigarette to my lips, stretching my fingers across the cocktail table towards an open book of matches that held a lone match-stick. Striking it against the black strip, the heat burned into my thumb, I inhaled deeply and let my shoulders sink back into the metal frame of the chair. An obviously inebriated, but happy looking couple stumbled through the door. Their initial bewilderment at having discovered the fire and dimly lit alcove was soon replaced by the giddiness of a shared secret. I observed them quietly until they noticed me- I'd almost hoped they wouldn't- it was creeping towards one o'clock and things would either pick up or continue to drawl by. Half of me had already mentally packed up and gone home. The woman's voice was shrill, but not overtly obnoxious and they wore matching bands on their ring fingers- these are the details you learn to look for. "Oooh, honey! Isn't she pretty?!" I allowed them to look me up and down. I was being sized up and priced- this was how the system worked.

I went back to enjoying my cigarette while the woman cooed and batted her eyes at her husband. They looked at one another excitedly before turning their gaze back to me; "Are you going to let me get naked and crawl all over you?" I offered sweetly. The man exchanged a glance with his wife before shoving a twenty dollar note into my palm. "Just her, I'll get caught up on the details later." He winked at the woman and she blushed a deep pink. I took her hand and led her back inside to the private dance room. She sat primly in the slouching chair, her palms pressed flat against the sticky vinyl, legs crossed, eyes drawn towards the floor- she peeked at me through her blonde fringed bangs. "Shhh, just relax- I know what I'm doing". I took her small hands and laced her fingers through mine, parting her legs gently with my knee, I slid my leg between her thighs and pressed my breasts against her sweater, inhaling deeply. She smelled sweet and musky. I exhaled heavily on her soft neck as she closed her eyes and her body went limp beneath me.

There are few things that I have experienced that are as gratifying as bringing a woman to orgasm: next to that was imagining bringing an otherwise seemingly straight woman to orgasm during a dance. I slid my body against her supple breasts. I imagined her with soft brown hair shorn close to her ears and small breasts with nipples that could cut diamonds. A soft moan escaped from her raspberry lips as I pulled the blue top over my head, licking my pointer finger and tracing the outside of my nipple. I envisioned this new woman prone, legs spread before me, caressing her inner thigh with my mouth, sucking the soft skin where thigh meets cunt, enveloping an engorged clitoris with my thirsty tongue, feeling her muscles contract around one, and then three fingers tighter and more frenzied with each thrust until my lips glistened with her musky wetness. The song ended and I opened my eyes to find the blonde woman, still clothed, out of breath and looking dazed. "Th-thank you" she stuttered. "That was amazing." I replied with a sideways smile and a nod, "My pleasure, I'm glad you enjoyed yourself." She placed another twenty dollars on the bench next to me before waving and stumbling out of the room.

I rushed down to the dressing room to change my now-wet panties before my name was called and I was due back on stage, bounding up the stairs and pointing out two short songs for the DJ to play for my final set of the night. I danced quickly and happily through the next five minutes and collected my ones at the end of the set, pulling my bottoms on as I waited for the next girl to take over on stage. I made my way toward the bar with whiskey on my mind. A gentlemen sat in the corner; even better if I didn't have to pay for my drink. He offered to buy my cocktail and the bartender waited for my order;he was a perfectly complimentary mix of stern and maternal. I asked for Bulleit on the rocks. She gave a quick nod and poured with the lightning speed that comes with having done something a thousand times.

I thanked her and turned toward the man. He offered his glass to toast. "To new beginnings- I just moved here three days ago." I welcomed him to Portland as our glasses clinked together, nudging the fat bottom on the bar for good luck. "Where did you grow up" he inquired. I took a long pull on my bourbon. The truth was I had grown up here- not here as in Portland, but *here* at this club. I thought back to my audition; I couldn't even look at myself in the mirror clothed, let alone enjoy the beauty of my figure nude in front of a dozen strangers. My voice would drop to a whisper when I spoke about sexuality. Even saying "sex" aloud was painful. It was here that I learned what it meant to be a woman, to claim space, the necessity of self-worth in the midst of a hundred hungry eyes. Here that I came to understand that there is no shame to be had in standing up for yourself, in testing your limits, in keeping yourself safe. Here, in the company of a dozen of the strongest women I had ever known, I finally fathomed the power held within womanhood. Something I was raised to fear, lest I be called out for shining too brightly or abandoned and accused of obstinence. Here, I learned to listen to myself and to trust. Here I learned that you'll never know where home might turn out to be. Whether they knew it or not, the women I danced with pulled me up and through them. I saw my strength, learned to wield it like a powerful weapon, to sing it like a melody, to walk in its rhythm and to dance with it every single day. Where was I from? "Oh, I'm from here" I replied. I felt the warm burn flow down into my belly as I swallowed the last of my whiskey. "Thanks for the drink, and welcome to Portland." I set my glass down and smiled.

Occupational Hazards

(A List of Injuries I've Incurred as a Stripper)

By Sarah Tressler
Fort Worth, Texas

- Bruises, bruises, bruises
- Broken toenails from sliding back on the tips of my shoes over a bump in the stage
- Broken acrylic nails from popping up too quickly from twerking on stage and catching my nail on a crack by the hydraulic platform
- A sprained neck from sliding off the pole upside down too fast and landing on my head
- A sprained ankle from tripping in 6-inch heels on uneven, tattered carpet
- Singed hair while I was doing a backbend from the stage over a candle
- Pole burn on my inner thighs from grasping on for dear life as I slid too quick for comfort from the top of a 12-foot brass pole
- Fabric burn from the armrests of old chairs, where I propped the backs of my thighs to keep my body from touching the customer's but still gave me maximum control

- Ridiculous toe callouses from where every stripper shoe ever made rubs the tops of your feet
- An unintended sunburn from tanning for work too long (and the possible skin cancer that may go along with that later)
- A too-robust dose of cynicism
- An unhealthy suspicion of abandonment, and …
- Bruises.

This one time, I almost peeled my toenail off my big toe while I was in front of an audience. I was in a top-of-the-pushup position on stage at Treasures and was sliding backwards on the fronts of my stiletto's platforms into a customer who was waiting at the rail, when my newly manicured toe caught on the vent in the stage floor that shoots out that smelly fog. I had tears in my eyes while I did my booty shake tip-me moves. The nail was still attached but broken and bleeding.

I mean, you get weird but frequent injuries as a stripper.

Girls at New York Dolls have to go on stage about eleventy times a night, so that means two things: first, they're in amazing freaking shape, like, for real. Don't start a fight with anyone. And secondly, anyone doing pole work is nailing their shins and thighs on the regular. The former was great: tight abs, butt, quads and calves. You're in good enough shape to try out for the New York City Corps de Ballet. (Maybe.) The latter, however, put a damper on the former, because you look like you're married to a midget who has a domestic abuse problem. Battered all up and down from knees to ankles. The solution? Tanning.

The solution, unfortunately, also caused a problem. Strippers tend to be tan anyway, so this wasn't much of a stretch, but the decision between getting a spray tan (or "spranning" as one girl called it) and roasting yourself alive in a tanning bed was where problems could occur. Spranning means you stink like teriyaki chicken, usually for a day or two, and it rubs off in patches where you sweat. Tanning in a bed means, you know, cancer, along with fresh new freckles and moles and "You're a doctor, can you look at these?" things on what had been previously otherwise unblemished (if however bruised) skin.

After one such fake tanning session I raised the lid, flopped sweatily out of the hard plastic bed and examined my naked body in the room's full-length mirror. I was developing an even bronze from clavicle to toes (I laid a tanning salon towel over my face and neck, creating the white-face-brown-body effect that requires using up tons of bronzer to even things out), but my bottom was straight burned- like, "looks like it might peel" burned. The cheeks glowed red, two large dots punctuating my body like a colon. Near my colon. This, however, was probably not the worst burn I've sustained as a stripper. (It may in fact be the worse burn I've sustained, but I won't know until I get through life without growing melanoma on my ass.)

Back bends are a thing to do on a big stage if you're a flexible dancer, since you're always looking for ways to give your ankles a break to keep from the dreaded wobbly-ankled runway crash. (More on this later.) So mid-backbend, I was confused when a trio at a table by the stage went from smiling and tipping to gasping and trying to hit me in the head. Turns out the little propane candles that provide that sensuous ambient strip-club lighting don't mix with hair or hair "product". My bangs had fallen into the candle and caught aflame. And while this could have been infinitely worse (I sustained no major burns, just the loss of some already too-long bangs), I was mortified. Seeing a girl slip and fall on stage is bad enough; it's so loud that everyone cranes around to see what happened, and you can't look sexy while you're taking a spill half-naked. Most people don't look tucked and toned when they're falling down. But catching your head on fire, well, there are worse ways to embarrass yourself on stage, but almost all of them involve an involuntary releasing of one or more anatomical sphincters.

Poles are sources of all kinds of danger. Pole burn- that nasty Indian-burn feeling on the insides of your thighs from sliding to fast- is pretty common and causes its own set of suspicious-looking bruises (and cuts, too, if you're wearing a bottom that's covered in sequins. The ones around your crotch can slice into that delicate inner-thigh skin with enough pressure). But the most dreaded pole injuries come from just plain falling off. You climbed too high because you had too many Starfucker energy drinks and Pucker shots, and now you think you can go all Cirque-du-Soleil on the pole. Sometimes that works out and it's great fun and you make a lot of money; good for you!

Sometimes you fall while you're hanging upside-down and land on your neck. And then sometimes after that you walk around looking like Frankenstein in heels because it hurts to move and you can't turn your neck in any direction, and then sometimes after that you realize that you're endangering the lives of small children and animals because you can't really look around while you're driving, and then sometimes after *that* you go to a shady Mexican chiropractor's office in an old house next to a used car dealership ("NO CREDIT, NO PROBLEM! HABLAMOS ESPANOL"), and then sometimes that chiropractor and his beautifully pregnant nurse/file clerk/receptionist shock you with weird little electrodes and then pull sharply on your head until you are sure you heard the sound of an egg cracking, and your neck vertebrae hurt like to the point where you saw little stars for a second, but now "it's much better, thanks. Here's your $40."

The injury you're most likely to see, though, is a girl tripping on stage. Something about a stage and 7-inch stilettos and mounds of naked flesh make for a truly tragic scene when a girl trips on stage. It's not unlike watching a coltish runway model lose purchase in a set of avant-garde couture platform pumps with a floating heel, or an inverted heel, or a missing heel, or whatever, go flop-crash during a fashion show. These otherwise beautiful, almost superhuman creatures are literally brought crashing down to earth, and it practically makes the ground shake and the record scratch but the song goes on, or the fashion show goes on, and you have to try to get up and make it look good because you just looked about as ridiculous as you're hopefully ever going to look on stage, and coming back from that is a chore to say the least. God forbid you actually break something in this manner. Nothing says "overdue rent" like a stripper being carried off the stage on a gurney. And then there are all the little things that add up, most of which involve the lower back, hips, knees, and especially, the feet.

I would like to momentarily recognize the makers of professional-grade stripper stilettos. There are two types of 6-to-7-inch heels that don't really hurt that bad, and they are either, a) shoes that fall into the "Premier Designer" section of the Saks Fifth Avenue website or other luxury-goods retail shop (and even then they have to be engineered well), or b) stripper shoes. The former cost upwards of $700, and the latter anywhere from $40 to $200, depending on how bedazzled you want to be. And the cheaper shoe here is way more comfortable. Yes, it's made from plastic and Lucite, but they're relatively lightweight and have an absorbent cushioned footbed, which frankly makes them comfortable enough to jog in or skip in. On stage. At the end of the night.

Nevertheless, wearing shoes that prop your foot at a 45-degree angles for hours on end, during which time you likely aren't sitting down to dinner or watching a show, or some such thing that women who wear $700 stilettos do when they're out wearing $700 stilettos, and instead running all over a strip club for hours and hours and actually having to balance your little ankles and adjust your posture and bend ever so slightly at the knee, and stay on your toes, and all the trappings that come from wearing shoes like this, et cetera, et cetera– it eventually causes funny things to happen; i.e., you get a weird frown-shaped crescent of callouses where the vamp rubs along the joints of your toes. Your spray tan rubs off under the vamp, causing a bizarre-looking white strip across the tops of your feet. Getting the shoes off at the end of the night when you're dying to just stand on the flat, solid floor is an exercise in caution and patience. The shoes are made to "stick" to your foot, which means you kind of have to pry them off, and then your toes are molded into the shape they've been in all night, and it takes a while for them to even separate, and it's almost kind of just like that scene in *Black Swan* where Natalie Portman starts growing webbed toes and has to pull them apart.

Plus, your ankles have to be coaxed back to their default position, because after a while, the 45-degree angle starts to feel like the default position. You find yourself wearing high wedges and those ridiculous high-heeled high-tops during the day, even to like, theme parks (not that I frequent those), because your Achilles tendon is used to being a tad shorter. So at the end of a night of work, you stand at your locker, balancing on your already-tired legs trying to scrape your heels off your now-swollen feet and when you get one off, you have to stand on one leg in a stiletto for long enough to allow your bare foot, which looks like it's been wadded up, to reform. But when you put your foot down, it's like having a tiny foot orgasm. Your feet spread; you feel like you have duck feet, like the tendons and bones that attach to your toes are being pulled apart by invisible magnets, like blood is rushing to parts of your feet that you didn't know existed, and now, *now, they are free,* so free – it just about makes your eyes roll back and your sphincter give, but at least you're not on stage, where everyone can watch it happen if in fact it does.

Audition Story

Casper Suicide
Portland, Oregon

I WAS NERVOUS.

For one, I had never even been inside of the business; I had heard stories, mostly bad, and the tall, old building with stone pillars and flickering red signs had sat there for decades, yet I have driven past it so many times and wondered what it would be like to enter.

The solid, serious man with SECURITY on his shirt was seated and looked very, very bored, yet intimidating, and unmistakably Russian. Its odd, but I could tell. He held our IDs under a blue scanner, and slowly placed them back within reach.

Um, I was wondering if I might audition, tonight? I chirped.

And I watched his eyes glance at my face, then glance just below, at the bulk (or lack) of my body. He gave a half nod, and indicated over his left shoulder.

In zeh cornerh, at zeh deejay booth

The Bearded One and I proceed to enter, and as I turn as see the most of the room, I am surprised, and impressed. It is smaller than I had expected, but everything looks shiny, and clean. Much cleaner than my previous club.

All of the girls are taller than me, and have much more makeup on than I usually wear. I see a smattering of tattoos, heels, and long hair. There is one cat-eyed black girl, with a blonde mini-afro. She looks bored. They all look a little bored. I wonder if I look like that when I'm at work at 9:40 on a Wednesday night.

We find a spot at the bar counter, furthest from the main stage, and I see H---- on the pole. She looks bored too. She flips from leg to leg, allowing the pole to hold her upside down; she runs a hand through her hair, as if she's never felt more relaxed. Its now that I recognize the song that is playing, the cover of Sir Mix a Lots Baby got back.

Okay, so. I survey the scene, I tell the Bearded One to please get me a tequila shot, and Ill be right back.

The place is nearly empty of customers, so when I spot Snuggy Guy immediately to my left, I tap his shoulder, and give him a big Hello and a Hug. I tell him that I'm auditioning, because, well the cats about to be outta the bag

At the DJ booth, the guy looks younger than DJ Robert, more "hip" but not in a good way, I'm pretty sure that I see pomade or some kind of gel in his dark hair. There is a tall, unfamiliar stripper, with sporadic black and white tattoos; I think its outlines of roses on her side and arm. long dark hair, and very heavy face and body makeup, talking to him. I stand behind her height, and wait for him to notice me, without interrupting.

When they both turn, I repeat my line to the DJ, Hello; I'd like to see about auditioning tonight?

He blinks, adjusts his vision to my face, and then I see him glance at my body. I might be as short as this man, but because he is in his booth, he is a foot taller. I look up, smiling, closed mouthed, hands folded in front of my waist.

I'm so demure.

Okay, (sighs) how long do you need to get ready.

Not a question, a statement.

I'm ready now, I just need to take my shirt off, and I can go up.

He surveys my outfit.

Dark brown cowboy boots with buckles, a leopard pencil skirt, and a black, loose fitting top with short sleeves. My hair is curled, but in short, low pigtails, and my straight bangs softly frame my eyes and cheeks. I'm still smiling at him. Demure, right?

Okay, you get one song, and it will be next. What song do you want.

Again, not a question.

The only band I name, he laughs and says he doesn't know what that is. I was prepared for this. I was also prepared for him laughing at me like I'm a newbie. Okay, next idea.

An explosion of blonde hair steps into view, and its Rocket! Glittery, tall, aggressive, take-no-prisoners, Rocket. I am the baby-stripper, and she is the Sage.

I have some Spinnerette you can use, on my iPod.

And I want to hug her. Its rare that another stripper, friend or not, will offer up her music. Suggestions are one thing, but off of her own iPod. I make a mental note, of this favor, and I thank her.

I return to the bar, and I tell the Bearded One, I'm up next. My tequila is waiting for me, and I see he has barely sipped his Newcastle. I shoot my drink and bite into the lime, sucking on the rind, and resisting the urge to chew that up and swallow it as well.

Bearded One asks if I want him to sit at the tipping rack. I think about it. I tell him that no, thank you, but Ill just do it.

And Hera's song winds down, and I step away from the bar, placing my clutch-wallet in his hands.

Ill be right back!

Walking toward the stage, its dark, there are three men at the rack, they look young, friendly, cheap, one has a hat, how do I get onstage? Oh, there's the opening, where's the rag to wipe, where's the spray, okay, I see the towel and bottle, goddamn that pole looks thicker than what I'm used to, Hera sees me and she looks pissed.

I smile, and greet my former nemesis, Hello, miss Hera.

And she grimaces, and covers her boobs and she scoots past me.

The DJ has announced that there is an audition, and I don't look up until I have wiped the enormous, unfamiliar pole, and tossed the rag in the corner of the stage.

Adrenaline floods my body, and I'm suddenly aware of how smooth the stage is. And I hear Brody Dalle, begin singing to me, and everyone else.

Have you ever been alone, fighting your own war...

I feel the warmth spread across my face, and I'm peeking out at the audience, underneath my heavy fringe. The men in front of me, are smiling, they look really pleased to be in the presence of someone who seems to be having fun. I love when I see that expression.

... Someone stole the life from you, and now they're back for more...

I see that every single person in the building has come to a halt, is frozen. Every other stripper has one hand holding a drink and the other rested on a hip. The bartenders are leaning on the counter. The Bouncer has turned around to watch. I can't see the Bearded One, but I know he's watching too.

...Your heart is on the floor, Beating out of control...

I love this song. I've never pole danced to it. I used to sing it to myself in tears, when I was driving in the dark, alone. I havent listened to it in a long time, but I still, really love this song.

...Oh, I don't want this anymore ...

My body kicks into gear, and I'm alive. I'm winding and lifting, and spinning, and slamming, kicking and twisting my legs around. My right nipple snags as I pull my bandeau top up, but I keep smiling and make a mental note to check for blood, later.

It is a few minutes like this, that I live for. The good outweighs the bad, when I feel this. The three minutes sail by.

I'm euphoric, I'm ecstatic. I want another song. But, I'm finished. I don't feel a thing, but I'm betting my knees will ache later. In the morning.

I crawl smoothly, across the floor, to collect my singles. I thank the two men, who are still smiling, and nodding. They tell me that I'm hired. I laugh, Thanks guys, I hope it's that simple!

As I leave the stage, I don't know where else to go, so I head towards the corner of the DJ booth. The girls who are still standing part for me, and a couple of them say some very kind words of encouragement, which I am grateful for. I'm wondering if any of them secretly hate me yet.

This time, the DJ looks at me differently, as he hands me some paperwork. I hear the words, amazing and perfect. I'm beside myself with pride. He tells me to follow him downstairs, and I do.

The dressing room is clean, red, and large. Lockers and clothing everywhere, and doors to closets(?) There is a girl I recognize, with big soft eyes; I can't remember her name, but when she sees me I greet her and ask how her daughter is. She seems tired, and I feel bad when I see that her stomach still indicates that she had a very large pregnancy. It was two years ago, but her loose skin and puckered stomach crave to be hidden by a waist-cincher. She was raised as a circus performer, and has stage abilities like Cirque du Soleil, yet her body hinders her from getting respect of club-owners.

There is a young looking, thin, blond-mohawked girl with her back to me, I recognize her from Dolphin. She looked pissed that night, eating her macaroni, and she looks pissed now.

DJ Jared tells me to read the paperwork, and to list what shifts I want. In caps, without hesitating, I print, Thursday Night and Saturday Night.

Awesome, if that's what you want, you pretty much have it. Here is the Owners card, call him right now, and tell him that I will text him your info within the next fifteen minutes.

And I do.

The Regular

Loren Hunt
Philadelphia, Pennsylvania

THE BAG IS huge and designer and made of deep green suede, of the recent era in which tiny starlets were often photographed dangling from their crooked elbow bags as big as their entire torsos. It is rigorously classic in style, made special back then by its lack of ostentatious logos or hardware or other whistles and bells. I don't remember the pretense under which my first regular bought it for me, only that I carried it everywhere I went for at least two years straight. It's held up well– the green suede mottled with use and the leather corners peeling just a little bit, but beautiful and bourgie-impressive as ever. The bag must be almost ten years old now and I still pull it out when I have a meeting or know I'll end up somewhere nice for lunch. This is how Jan knows it's me after all this time; he'd been proud enough of that purchase to recognize it from across the street.

I've given lap dances to so many middle aged men in this city that now every middle-aged man looks vaguely familiar. Therefore, I never really look at any of them, lest they end up wanting something from me during my off-duty hours. I don't strip anymore, but what was once a justifiable self-preservation tactic is now simply a vestigial habit. Once, over a summer break, I ran into the (male, middle aged) dean of my department in a convenience store and returned his greeting with the evasive half-smile reserved for customers, only to realize fifteen minutes later who I'd just blown off. But Jan is, even years later, physically specific. He got me early, back when customers still had faces, before I learned how to work without breaking off a piece of myself for every man who thought he wanted one. He's as immediate and undeniable from across the street as if he'd been a real boyfriend or lover or long-lost friend.

I had to bend down to hug Jan when I wore stripper heels, but in the flat Bass sandals I put on this morning, we are exactly the same height. Jan is one of those men who carry all their weight in the middle, giving the appearance of being as wide as they are tall. He's freckled and balding, with a twinkly earring in one ear and a yellow shirt with rolled-up sleeves. He looks somewhere between someone's idea of a sleazy Hollywood producer and what he actually is, an east coast corporate lawyer. Jan hasn't changed much from the days when I was his steady date.

"You look great," he tells me and I wonder how sincere this is. I definitely look different than I did six or seven years ago: an extra fifteen pounds, a wash-and-wear hairstyle in my natural color, glasses, a more conservative wardrobe, ragged cuticles. My outward appearance finally matches who I am— a spinstery, bookish sort. Not gross or anything, but no one's idea of paid arm candy.

It's only maybe 2 PM, but we end up drinking vodka sodas in the bar of the Steven Starr joint close to where we met on the street. "You're a professor!" he crows when I tell him what I'm doing with my life. "That's terrific! If your students only knew."

"I'm just an adjunct," I say, smiling, so proud of my job that I even get a thrill out of deprecating it. Having stripped for six years, the privilege of being able to tell people what I do for a living without causing them to picture me naked is one that I bask in. Jan is looking at me like he thinks we should have more to say to each other, so I tell him that. But even saying the word "naked" feels like an undesirable provocation. I change the subject: "how is your family?"

When I met Jan, I was about a week into being allowed to work night shifts at Wizzards, my first club. Seeing as I was so naïve I'd shown up for my audition dressed in job interview clothes, complete with nude pantyhose, I cut my teeth on day shifts for a month, and it was a good thing I had– everything about the strip club was completely foreign to me. The stimulation of night shifts even at a semi-dive like Wizzards might have otherwise undone me. For a long time, the only solid rules I heard were things like, "mind your business," "it takes money to make money," and, "you're here to make money, not friends." It wasn't until I was actually in a couch dance room giving one that I understood what I was supposed to do for $20 a song. But I found that I had a real taste for stripping, if not a natural knack; it was the most exciting thing I'd ever done. I was up close and personal with people I'd never had access to before and I found it exhilarating. My whole life was suddenly suffused with black lights and neon, throbbing bass lines, tickly biker beards, fake rhinestone jewelry, and vanilla-scented body spray.

Jan stuffed my pale blue satin bikini full of ones when I got off stage that night and told me he liked me. Later that night, he spent a couple hundred bucks on dances. The next time I saw him, I knew enough to go over and sit with him for a while. We talked and he told me that despite his Scandinavian sounding name (surname Petersen, two E's), he was a New York Jew whose father had been so obsessed with not appearing to be Jewish that he'd changed the family name. He told me, as an illustrative example of his father's obsession, that he'd grown up in a house with many Kiehl's products. I didn't really understand the correlation but this caught my attention, as the highly particular often does. Without giving it much thought, I switched over from stripper patter into a writer's interrogation and when he asked what I did, I admitted my daylight ambitions. This is how Jan got me; he told me he was looking to hire someone to turn a great-uncle's journals into a biography. Then he gave me a bunch of money. Of course I believed him. We exchanged numbers.

When we met up for an early dinner the following week, the writing project was not brought up again. But I meanwhile I had crab soup and a steak and few glasses of wine and crème brulee for dessert, as well as a $100 Victoria's Secret gift card for my time. I hadn't forgotten that we were meant to be discussing a potential job, but I let it slide. He dropped me off with a kiss on the cheek and a full belly. I was mostly grateful.

I was grateful the next week, too, when after a big fight with the guy I was seeing, I woke up hungover and heartsick to Jan's voice on the phone: "I reserved you a lobster at the Palm."

"I don't know about lunch, today, Jan. I'm hungover. I'm dealing with some stuff. I don't think I can put in the effort required of looking cute enough to go eat lobster."

"You can wear sweatpants and not shower for all I care. You will always be beautiful to me."

And these are cheap words, pat ones, the words expected from a person who wants to give the appearance that their desire is pure and unequivocal when it isn't. I had no intentions of ever sleeping with Jan, having a relationship with him, being his mistress. He was not particularly fooling me. But even in the state I was in, I could see the appeal of allowing myself to be cheered up. Lobster in sweatpants would probably do the trick.

It did that day, and it did repeatedly. I love good food more than feq things on this earth and Jan was great dining company, always encouraging me to order two appetizers if I wanted to try them both and never letting me skip dessert. We fell into a routine of going out to dinner about once a week. He'd bring me gifts— sometimes things I wanted, sometimes things he just thought I should have. Then he'd visit me in the club when I was working.

It was only when giving Jan lap dances in the back room that I felt the full weight and truth of what our relationship was about. Most of the time he felt like some kind of mildly inappropriate, extra-doting uncle, but the occasions when I found myself leaning over with him with my boobs in his face punctured that fantasy entirely. Having spent so much time with him, his touch and presence and arousal felt more personal than they usually did at the strip club, which forced me to navigate an uncomfortable territory in which I was most definitely doing something I didn't want to do. And for his favor. For money, really. The genuine affection we shared across the table at some nice restaurant made the false intimacy of a lap dance grotesque.

One night I felt his hand scrabbling over a section of my back that must have had some flaw, some pimple or scab, picking at it. I snapped. "Stop that!" My voice was loud and harsh and we both recoiled from each other, shocked.

We recovered from this right away, laughing it off and having a few drinks instead, but after that we stopped doing lap dances. He'd just hand me the money he used to spend on dances when he came in for a visit and we'd talk instead.

"The family is good. We sent JJ off to Smith a few years ago and she seems happy. She wants to be a photojournalist. The house is very quiet without her," Jan says. I used to be jealous of JJ, of all the presents he'd tell me he'd bought her: Chanel sunglasses, Marc Jacobs dresses, a car for her sixteenth birthday, various trips to European countries. JJ had the life. "I got a bunch of new musical instruments and I go down in the basement and play them a lot," he says. "Fire up a doobie, have a few beers, and just rock out."

"Do you still go to the club?" I want to know. Jan glances over at my drink before ordering himself another. "Sure, sometimes. I've had a few buddies there over the years. I'm trying not to get back into any bad habits, though, so I don't go as much anymore."

"That's good," I say, nodding. He's talking about cocaine, which he used to like a lot. I never saw him do any, but I don't think he'd have done it in front of me. He could have been using the bathroom. "I think I saw you and your family one night a few years back," I say. "You were walking right along Rittenhouse Square, probably coming from dinner."

"Oh, yeah?" he says, raising his eyebrows. "I didn't see you."

"You wouldn't have said anything if you did." I can't help it, it comes out kind of plaintive. The three of them had looked like they belonged together; all well turned-out, all distracted. Jan had either not seen me, not recognized me, or ignored me. I averted my eyes despite being madly curious about these people; Jan's real people. I wondered for the millionth time how he managed to hide his strip club habit, his drinking, his drugs– or if he even bothered, if maybe no one cared what he did anymore. I wondered where he'd told them he was going when we went out together. I wondered if they missed him, worried about him, let him have his foibles to ensure that he would come back to them at the end of it all. Worse, Jan made me wonder about my own dad– how well I really knew him, if he was happy, if he had a whole secret life I'd never know about.

"If I saw you walking on the street with a boyfriend or husband or something I would probably assume you didn't want to explain how you knew me," he says.

"No, Jan, I get it. It's okay. It is all totally okay."

These are some of the things Jan gave me over the six months or so that he was my benefactor: a pair of screwback diamond stud earrings, a set of bright red towels, a squishy feather pillow, a tiny flashlight that attached to my keychain, three cashmere sweaters from Nordstrom's, a hardcover copy of Dan Brown's "The DaVinci Code" with nice reproductions of all the art involved in the plot, a limited edition iPod engraved with the signatures of the members of the band U2, Narciso Rodriguez For Her perfume, Chanel Coco Mademoiselle perfume, Chanel No. 5 Elixir Sensuel perfume, a neon orange nylon change purse with a bunch of pockets for cards, a pair of high heels so expensive and spindly I was mostly afraid to wear them out of the house, a Swiss Army knife, a bunch of stripper costumes, and a red suitcase to pack my things in when I left Philadelphia to spend January and February in Charleston, South Carolina, where it was much warmer.

In Charleston, I stayed with Lou, a friend who'd known me since I was a teenager and supported my writing enough to loan me his couch for two months. He, like most of my friends, got a big kick out of the idea of me as a stripper. I think Lou finally understood the reality of that part of my life when, on Valentine's Day, an enormous arrangement of phalaenopsis orchids arrived at the house. There must have been fifty or more stems; showy even for Jan. They took up the entire coffee table and looked amusingly out of place against all the high bohemian junk that Lou had in his apartment. I called Jan and thanked him. Then I spent the next two weeks hoping the orchids would hurry up and die faster. Between bouts of writing, I'd lie on the couch and stare at them, sterile and styrofoamy, wondering if someone I actually liked would ever send me flowers I actually liked and hoping I was not ruining my chances of that forever by dancing in bars and knowing people like Jan. The orchids didn't seem like the sweet gesture they might have been under other circumstances: they seemed to be about insinuation and access and control.

They were a big arrangement of gently bobbing intruders, a gift from a man who did not know me and didn't really care to.

As it turned out, the orchids were also about guilt. While I was gone, Jan took up with my good friend Stella, who worked at the same club. He tried to make this okay for me by taking both of us out to dinner a few times after I returned from Charleston, but the writing was on the wall. What made matters even more annoying was that she knew everything I'd told her about him so was able to immediately one-up me in terms of asking for and receiving gifts that she actually wanted. It's such a bratty thing to pout over– you stole my no-sex sugar daddy!– and Stella was otherwise a good friend, so I never expressed more than mild displeasure to either of them. But I missed my weekend lobster lunches, it sucked to hear her plotting out his next purchases, and the thing that really burned my ass was that she pulled the whole thing off without ever once giving him a lap dance. I'd made it so easy for her that I wondered if I'd been unconsciously complicit in handing him over. Ultimately, it was a relief to let him go.

"Do you want to go outside and smoke with me?" Jan asks, pulling a pack of cigarettes from his pocket and tapping it against the palm of his hand.

"I quit," I say. "Maybe a year ago now. It sucked."

"Wow, you really are all grown up now." Jan decides to hold off on smoking for a while longer yet, ordering a third drink from the bartender. I'm not a slow drinker, and still on my first.

"Oh my God, you are going to die," I say. I'd meant it to come out a breezy joke, but a complicated flicker of emotions crosses his face and he looks away. "Probably," he says, flashing an insincere smile. We suck down the remainder of our drinks in an uncomfortable tandem and Jan asks the bartender for the check.

"It was so good to see you," I tell him, giving him another hug on the sidewalk. Jan lights up a Marlboro Light with shaking hands, hands that I remember have always shaken like that. But we don't exchange information, or make plans to do it again sometime. When I turn away from him to begin my long walk home, I feel the sunshine on my arms as a comfort, a reminder of the simplicity of my life these days. It's a simplicity I couldn't have chosen for myself had I not been fully aware of the alternative.

The handbag Jan gave me swings comfortably at my side. I've been carrying it for so long that I'd almost forgotten where it came from. For a few minutes, I'm full of plans to buy myself a new one with my own money, a handbag without any memories attached to it, one that some old guy across the street could never recognize as his. But I never do. I like this one.

I earned it.

Strip Story

Katie B.
Portland, Oregon

Peel away my clothes
Until you see only my naked body
One by one
Top.
Bottom.
Leave on the stage make-up,
The shoes that are too tall;
Leave the rest:
My small tits
my luscious pussy
my curvy ass
My ESSENCE is shining
The core of me
Is Complete
Strip it all away
peel me, like an onion
I am there
Burning, brighter and brighter.
Stronger.

It first started
at the Acropolis, a true Portland icon
"Hey, Dad, you ever been there?"
silence, like Normal
my Mom chiming in and taking over, like Normal
"Katherine! No! Strip clubs are
degrading, objectifying" and on and on and on
I've heard it all a million times
We went there, my beau and a somewhat current lover of ours
It was Sunday evening
we walked from our duplex, around the block
summer time
it was slow
the strawberries were moldy
our lover was uneasy,
and we left.
But I was entranced.
I could have stayed all evening.

But, really, it first started when I was
Born.
Alive.
Sexual.
Ready.
Molded.
Creating.
Taking.
Wanting.
Needing.
    connection, validation, support, intimacy.

Some people find these things through being the
Good Daughter
I had done that already

Some people find these things through
going through Life in a
straight (boring) line—
I never planned to do that
That's not why I moved to Berkeley for college
and it wasn't ever in my cards

Do you ever have that feeling
that somehow your life is unfolding
and you're just watching? marveling at the mystery? laughing at the novelty of it all?
You're doing what now, Self?
Stripping.
Stripping?
Stripping.
Okay, then. Let me grab some popcorn, 'cause this is going to be
Entertaining.
    [all with the caveat
    that this is my account from today,
    not yesterday and not tomorrow.
    details shift and change as I remember and forget and
    Remember.]

From my first audition at Blush
the slow club up the road
the DJ, high and belligerent
my Realization that this was a whole lot easier than I could have imagined
He came with me
because he is Amazing and Supportive and
All of the Things You Want Your Best Friend to Be
I wore my new outfit: Mary Jane dance shoes, black booty shorts, matching black string top
We left

my sense of self, jubilant
You did it.
I yelled inside

Lucky Devil was an unexpected blessing
(despite my near-constant complaints of management or
of tipping out or of the few fellow dancers
who were too stoned or high to know when
it was their turn to get on stage)
the smallness
the mellowness
the autonomy over my outfits and music
the ability to work on schoolwork and personal projects during downtime
the stage became my canvas, my therapy couch, my stretching-into-adulthood
the mirror became my best friend, my enemy, and my savior
the red glass and lights
turning everything into
an apocalyptic landscape
and covering up all external
blemishes
from the first two women I worked with at Devil's Point—Puff and a small Brazilian woman who could make fantastical shapes with her body—to the many at Lucky Devil, I was enthralled by the
enthusiasm and gall
of the wonderfully wicked women I worked with
the college students, the grad students, the med students, the moms, the teachers, the hairdressers, the estheticians, the activists, the writers.

"Has this place taught you anything about men?"
he asks me this a lot—one of my regulars.
No, I reply.
There are so many different kinds. If anything, I now have more categories of Men than I did before

those who want therapists, those who want friends, those who want lovers, those who just want to see a
Pussy
or to drink a beer in peace
those who want to come in
with their 20 guy friends to Parade Their Masculinity
Sitting at the stage, throwing down money, talking and laughing with each other, but not
Looking at You
because if they did, it would show everyone they don't have as much
Power
as they like to think they do.
there are the rare few
who have come in
and truly
Caught my Eye.
The handsome stranger who gave me genuine and Rapturous Smiles
the whole time he sat at my stage. Nine minutes and thirty nine seconds of
Bliss.
I wished I had given him my number.
The bar regular, who in any other context was
Not My Type,
but when I gave him private dances,
became my Adonis.
his curly hair and sweet smile and round face and strong, rough hands.
I wanted him.
I haven't seen him in a long while, and I wonder where he is.
Sometimes, this creeps into worry.
You want a therapist? Tell me all about your horribly traumatic childhood, from the terrible
Sexual Abuse
to the time you

Murdered someone
I have kept it all in, until I realize,
over a year later,
that I am a ~~victim~~ survivor of vicarious trauma.
So much toxicity
So much pain
You tell me that you use my face and my smile in your healing process,
plastering my image over your horrendous memories
You request private dances during which I simply
Sit in your lap
Stroke your bald head
and Gently caress your face
I comply
You are kind to me, for which I am grateful
I feel honored to be part of your story
    [And yet, I feel burnt out
    Likely how social workers feel burnt out
    which stops me a minute from progressing in my plans to become one]
You made me a beautiful coffee table,
("I want to make you something beautiful," you told me, "to thank you")
steel, stained a gorgeous bright cherry color
the thick marble slab, I call it "Starry Night" for its swirls of gray, silver, navy, and gold
the bottom design you named "the poly" for its set of three rectangles
You have both seen me and Seen me and I appreciate the complexity of our
strange relationship.
There are others, though—other customers
the disgusting Pervert, the only one in a year and a half, who actually instilled a sense of degradation in
Me
a feeling I loathed
and I hated him for it

STRANGE TIMES

He told me how he fucked a dancer in the bathroom
and wanted to do it again
He stared angrily, stonily at my pussy
said some other derogatory things
and gave me
One Dollar
I didn't even want it.
There were many drinkers and smokers (of many varieties)—which put me at a
disadvantage for making Money, since I never smoke and
drink rarely.
There were homophobes and racists, and I
Despised
being in the club when I encountered socially backwards people.
Perhaps my favorite, though:
The kind, older Black man
who constantly talked about his wife
he brought in pictures of her
She is Lovely
told me several times about how his visits to strip clubs
taught him how to respect Women
that they are to be honored and revered
he paid me well, when
he had the money.
And when he came in just a month ago and told me his beautiful Maggie had died,
it brought tears to my eyes

I tried working at Casa Diablo
it was my favorite club as a customer
Girl-on-girl sex?!, my pussy quivered.
Acrobatic, performance-oriented, long-legged, long hair
I loved it all, I loved them all

I should try to work there
Two weeks and I had tried it
After an assault, I was done
We were going at it, I was going down on
Her
on stage
She was cute, but straight
but for the Money, she thought it would be fun Enough with me
The other girl, at the other end of the stage, was
Pissed
Came by, grabbed my friend's hair, and shook her hard
My mouth agape, I was speechless
what was this?
I never went back to work there.
The owner of the club auditions every girl himself. You must sit on his lap and let him
Touch You
so you know what the two-way touching lap dances are like
I have nothing against two-way touching lap dances, but I do have something against
Oppressive Use of Power
Once, when I was getting ready in the dressing room
I thought I was by myself
I look up, and a girl emerges from his closed office
Sex flush—chest, face, back
She walks quickly out
Says Thank You for letting her leave her shift early without paying the fee
His face looks contented, and it sickens me
    [Is this my own judgment?
    Is it possible that this dancer felt
    Empowered to use her body to her advantage even further?
    it is possible.
    the narrative of this story is mine, not hers.

STRANGE TIMES

For all I know, this woman
had it all Right.
    It is also possible, that my eyes
Made up the whole Thing,
creating a story congruent with how I viewed that
man- manipulative, abusive, and
Controlling.]

I had a crush on a bartender
My recently discovered Gay Side had taken full
Force when I met You
Your dreads
Your tattoos
Your curvy figure, your wide smile, your laugh
I was infatuated, for a
time.
We flirted.
you once made me a strong margarita,
knowing how much of a lightweight I am.
I told you that I might kiss you if I got too
Tipsy, and I think you wanted that.
You sat at my stage
Once.
And your eyes, looked…
so
Faraway.
Were you there?
I think so.
It was That Look.
I wanted you.
And even now, writing this, I want you. Or more truly,
the idea of you.
Because what happened between us has never been

repaired.
It was a terribly, sickeningly slow Sunday evening.
I had $20 after four and a half hours.
And my stomach hurt.
I needed to leave.
You told me No.
I dressed out anyway, determined to take care of
Myself
and not the Empty Club
You gave me the hardest glare, which
hardened to Steel
when you felt the
one dollar
I gave you as a tip for
Nothing.
My Crush on you has been gone since then
And our relationship replaced by iciness, reduced to coolness over time
Polite.
Like work relationships should be.
But the history of the flame, and the flame-out, remains,
forever reminding me to look
Behind the smile and laugh
to not be beguiled by my lustfulness
for a taste of Sweet Lips

Speaking of Tip Outs,
there's not a better way for me to self-induce High Blood Pressure.
How are clubs able to attract customers to their bars, to buy their drinks
and eat their food?
Naked Girls.
Who should be paying who, exactly?
Independent Contractors, my ass.
My club is better than others, so I hear

And I understand paying to work in a space if I truly am an
Independent Contractor
but whose job is it to make sure that
Your Staff
is paid adequately?
You, the Management. It's on you.
It's not the getting naked and performing for strangers that is oppressive.
It's the structure of the Strip Club,
set up so that wages are reorganized around the Men in the club, or those who are Employees.
People are willing to
Pay Me for my performance and company
My energy and time tonight earned me
$243.
Why on god's green earth does that mean I must give the DJ $20 and the bouncer $15 and the bartender $10?
Because on the earth where
Patriarchy has Dominated,
women must necessarily be below, beneath
and if now they are Empowered to be naked, profiting from their grandiose naked brilliance,
why they must *pay for it*.
Ten percent please, to each.

Getting Ready
consists of shower and make up
Black eyeliner to make my blue eyes Pop
Pheromones perfume
    [I had been sold on this stuff a while back
    at a friend's Pure Romance party
    Did you know
    that it *actually* smells
    Different on Different People?

     Citrusy and sweet on my wrist?
     Musky and dark on my friend's?
     I don't know if it ever made a difference
     in how people treated me or how much
       Money I made
     But it was my best friend at work]
My favorite outfit:
$74 bejeweled five inch heels, with a zipper closure at the heal, peep toes
A strappy "dress" which shows off my curvalicious ass
and my
"Vajazzle"
—which should be my Trademark—
black g string with a large jewel that covers the front of my
pussy
"Does that hurt?" people ask
Why would I wear something that hurts?
No, it's just hot.
Bath and body works perfume complete me at work
Feeling scented and done
Covered and yet
Not covered at
all.
Every twenty to thirty minutes
I dance
     [I am completely taken over, and often lose
     track of all time.
     I am consumed by my own energy
     though I play off of others', if it is
     positive or playful or hot.
     I distance and stay within my bubble if the energy
     is tired or bored or haughty.
          Although I would be Lying if I
          tried to pretend that low or gross energy doesn't

    impact me while I dance.
    it can weigh me down, until I
    feel Depleted.]
peel off my dress and my g string
leaving myself naked, but not
Naked.
    [sometimes, I do
    get Naked for someone while I dance.
    usually, for the Loves in my life
        who have frequently graced my stage]
When I get home, I get truly
Naked.
Running a hot bath, pouring Epsom salt
waiting for the magical properties to take
my body over.
renewed, relaxed, and
ready for the next.

Body image
Issues
have plagued me since I was about seven years old.
I carried a lot of baby fat through elementary school
feeling Fat and Fatter than all of my friends
I had my last growth spurt at 12
And suddenly I felt
Skinny
which equaled/s
Being Worthy (of love, appreciation, respect)
And the Hyper-vigilance began
when might the weight return?
the extra fat around my stomach and butt and thighs?
I kept myself hungry throughout high school,
priding myself on going to bed starving and eating small

amounts of food
at dinner.
When I began exercising in college,
and fell in Love,
I began eating more, my curves
filling out More.
I became More.
And the hyper-vigilance cranked up
and continues on.
At times,
dancing has helped me
feel beautiful and worthy and sexy
and at other times,
dancing has worsened my
Anxiety and Self-Shaming
as I watch my curves in the mirror,
trying to pray away my god-given shape and size
No amount of Hollow Flattery
or even Genuine Desire and Admiration
can ease the pain
It must come from inside, a
Recognition and Belief
that I am Worthy of love and belonging
simply because I am alive
and here.

"Do your parents know that you dance?"
For fuck's sake, what do you think?
"Katherine! No! Strip clubs are
degrading, objectifying" and on and on and on
I've heard it all a million times,
Like I mentioned before.
I'm a third-waver

Women can enjoy rape fantasies
they can enjoy submissive sex
they can be sex workers
and women can demand equality
and they can demand equity
They can demand an end to sexual violence
they can demand reproductive rights and medical coverage
they can be anti-sex trafficking activists
(Because consciously chosen sex work is a world apart
from
sex trafficking.)
My mom, on the other hand,
comes from a place that taught her, through childhood molestation, that sex always goes with monogamy, it always goes with love, and it always goes with spirituality.
Pornography, sex work, casual sex
these things are Outside Her Scope
and that's okay.
It's understandable
> [I like to think that all of my sexual experiences have been part of a larger Cosmic Plan to heal from my family lineage.
> From the time I had sex consensually at age 15
> to my explorations outside of monogamy and
> straighty-straight land
> to my Buffet of Stripping Delights,
> I see myself healing, from
> The Inside Out,
> the legacy of sexual violence and
> trauma, the
> experiences of which
> have been sewn into my cells and DNA,
> into the fibers of my being,
> which hears and sees the potential for terror

and sadness and violence
around every corner.
Sometimes I am amazed I am not more paranoid
than I am.]
We are different people
But it's a difference I fear she would not be able to get past readily
the relationship between her and I is already somewhat fragile
I listen and respond tenderly, gingerly—although
sometimes rudely and curtly—and yet always aware
of the fragility, knowing when to show my real
Thoughts
and when to acquiesce to hers.
"Do you have enough money? How are you two making it?"
I cannot lie. I am terrible at lying.
I tell her it's fine, that I'll ask if I need anything.
The façade that I create—that I don't work at all—is almost more painful
to tend to, I think,
than had I told the Truth.
His parents deal with this story more rudely than my parents
Seeing my "not working" as laziness
they cannot get past it
Somehow, someone, somewhere tells his mom that I am a stripper
but she hasn't brought herself to actually ask him or I
about it.
I would tell her the Truth now.
But instead of The Truth cracking her stereotypes about all strippers having
Damaged Psyches
I am pretty sure she would just start viewing me as a poor girl
with a Damaged Psyche,
furthering her case that her Golden Boy should
find someone else.
So I leave

the Parents Out of It.
    [and maybe in some distant Future
    or some parallel universe—there is speculation now in the
    physics circle that this could actually exist—
    I tell my parents, in an offhand way.
    When these years come up in conversation:
    "Remember when you didn't work? How hard that was?"
    No, I worked. I was a stripper.
    Mouths open, dumbfounded.
    And because so much Time has
    gone by,
    there is far less conversation about it.
    Just a passing story about my
    early twenties, a link in
    the chain of my existence
    easier to explain in that way
    than while I am in the active Process
    of crafting and integrating it
    within Myself.]

I am White and
Upper Middle Class and Educated and
Temporarily Able Bodied and
Attractive and
Partnered to a Man
I am Privileged with a
Capital P
I share my story with others,
feeling some fear that I will be judged or
ostracized
but I also remember
that these feelings are nothing compared
to the discrimination and

marginalization that
impact so many
every day
my womanness and queerness and nonmonogamousness and stripperness
allow me to feel
oppressed at times
but I am Buffered beautifully
by all of my Capital positions
the stress I feel from my smallness can be high for me sometimes
but in the grand scheme of the human experience
it is so low,
so very, very low.
This is part of my motivation to
share my story
to help break stereotypes
to talk about marginalized communities
so that those with Power
may listen and begin
to understand.

I am more than
Stripper.
I have a college degree
and a masters degree.
I am queer.
and love nonmonogamy and certain kinky things.
I have a miniature labradoodle
and a Partner that I Love.
I love baking and blogging and reading
and exercising
Until I Sweat Through Everything I Own.
I love backpacking and turning off my
cell phone and computer

I am spiritual—believing
Everything Happens for a Reason
I decided I wanted to become a therapist.
So I went back to school,
entranced with the training and the schoolwork,
determined to get through the program
As All of Me.
Including the Stripper-Part-Of-Me.
I do it. I tell a group of
Strangers
that I am a Stripper.
some thank me privately
some thank me publicly
some tell me that I helped them
break down Stereotypes of what being a stripper
Means
One classmate confides in me that she, too, has a history of
dancing
She feels comfortable being there, knowing of my experiences.
And then:
Oppressive Use of Power.
Veiled behind Academics and Ethics,
faculty convene at the request of one professor.
Tell me that stripping violates the Holy Code of Ethics.
Tell me that stripping is not "the issue"
Tell me that I cannot both be an ethical therapist-in-training
and a stripper
So Stripping *is* The Issue
Tell me that stripping may contribute to
"further injustice in the world"
I am furious
FUCK YOU, I write in a blog post as I sit in the strip club
I am disheartened

I am in disbelief
I am sad
I Grieve
I leave.
Fuck you, I say.
I fantasize about other ways, more interesting and extraordinary ways, this particular part of
My Story
happened.
I think about this person
walking into my club
late one day, after work.
Doesn't see me there until she is drunk.
She buys a dance from me and tries to
Touch Me
I tell her No and
she stops, sadly.
She hands me a wad of money and stumbles out before I have a chance
to Count it and realize
she has given me one hundred dollars
for one dance.
I race to the front but she is gone.
She is the Fool.
Or, another way:
as the Treacherous Snake,
she becomes obsessed with me, after
seeing me dance once night.
She stalks me, follows me home.
As I get out of my car she tries to grab my arm,
but I have my pepper spray
Ready
And she falls
My heart racing, and my whole body

Shaking,
I call the cops.
With another ending and a different fantasy, I kill her as the Vengeful
Protagonist. In some sort of
Morbid, dark story about a stripper who lures a cranky, backwards
professor into her dark basement for some private tutoring—
and then—
BAM! she's gone.
    [perhaps in all of these, I am
    the Vengeful Protagonist?]
Now, I actually see her as some sort of mystical benefactor in my
Grand Life Story.
She pushed me out of the place I had gone to,
to become a therapist for those who are on the edges
of society.
She pushed me out, but I am making my way more rapidly and
Strongly than
even I thought I would.
It's all happening, with or without her.
It's all happening, because this,
this is
Mine.

My Therapist
has a special vantage point into these experiences of mine:
You want to be seen and to be heard. Do you think
perhaps
in that slow, trying-to-make-you-think-it-was-all-your-idea-kind-of-way
dancing has given you that? To be seen and to be heard?
Well, sure.
I am seen and heard, and in that sense,
I am powerful.
That could be the psychoanalytical interpretation, if you are my psychotherapist

who has seen the darkest parts of my brain for over a year and a half.
But the start had so much more to do with
Movement
and Flexibility
and performance
and My Sexuality
the orange, pleasure chakra
bouncing and spinning around, out of control
women, naked women
exhibitionism
sensuality
oozing all day, every day
Those were my driving factors
I see my therapist's point, the idea
that stripping has fed my need for
People to see me
But few have *actually* Seen Me
And this I am aware of
For I am not stripper
And yet I am *all* stripper
And to peel away one layer, leaves
one with another
and to spend the time,
crying and laughing
to really know and understand
takes time and Effort
and few have the muscle
and the desire to do that
Especially
When what most want
is to be sold a Fantasy
to Desire something outside of their
Reach.

STRANGE TIMES

The beginning is the end and
the end is the beginning.
Ouroboros.
The more time I spend,
trying to understand myself,
the more tired I become. Until I give up,
for now.
And I move on, until something tomorrow
prompts me to look inward once again, delving into
the mysteries.
Stripping has been a rich avenue for this
Exploration.
It's one experience, among an infinite array in human lives.
And I am blessed and
Grateful
to have it as part of my Story.

Doggy Style

Nikki
Oregon

THE FIRST STRIP club I ever worked at was less of a club and more of a hole in the wall. It was located on the industrial waterfront, and most of the customers were steel workers or longshoremen. They called it The Clubhouse, and every weekday it would be crowded with men in dirty work clothes ready for a beer and a burger. The girls were an afterthought.

I had previously auditioned at one other club and got a "Don't call us; we'll call you." I brought the stripper heels I had been practicing in at home, but when I got there my legs were shaking so badly I just wore my busted black leather combat boots on stage. I was nervous as fuck. My audience consisted of one disaffected Asian man with nowhere better to be than the strip club at 2PM on a Sunday. As he watched me trip out of my panties and try not to fall off the stage he looked so bored he might as well have been staring at the wall. The manager was a shriveled leathery woman who played video lottery through my entire audition, glancing up once or twice to witness my humiliation.

It was early December. I had just finished college and was completely broke. During school I worked as a phone sex operator for several years—a whole different story—but I was really burnt out on it. Sick of being stuck alone in my apartment in front of a computer, I wanted to branch out into a different kind of sex work. After I completely bombed my first audition, a friend of mine told me about The Clubhouse, and rode down there with me on that fateful Tuesday afternoon. I felt just as awkward as before, but the female booking agent hired me on sight. They were short a dancer (three girls worked each shift), so I was invited to stay and work right away.

The music came from a dilapidated jukebox with the most insane collection of songs ever assembled in a strip club. The owner was a woman in her sixties who had a strict rule of no cursing in her establishment. This went for the staff whenever she was around, as well as the music we were allowed to play. Her tastes combined with the lead bartender's to dictate our selections. Every Jimmy Buffet CD ever made, three Toby Keith albums, Metallica's Black Album, a variety of Greatest Hits, including Judas Priest, Ozzy Osbourne, The Rolling Stones, and the Wedding Singer Soundtrack were some of the highlights. To this day every time I hear "Pass the Dutchie" I get a weird, Pavlovian instinct to take off all my clothes.

The Clubhouse had one stage and offered no private dances. The stage itself was as long and narrow as a canoe, the back of it a mirrored wall split by one wooden column in the center. There were a couple of cracks in the mirror, and a "No Bad Days" palm tree sticker I assumed was another token of the owner's fanatic love for Jimmy Buffet. Their version of a stripper pole was an awkward handicap rail bolted into that center column, and to this day I don't know what they expected us to do with it. I saw more than one girl use it to launch themselves upside-down on the ceiling like a naked Spiderman, but it never looked sexy. Old beer lights and sports collectables covered the ceiling. A cardboard likeness of Betty Boop à la *Seven Year Itch* stood next to the stage. Below that was a hand painted sign that looked about thirty years old, reading "Dancers Work For Tips Only/ No Touching."

After being hired in my street clothes, I was shown the "dressing room," a.k.a. the women's bathroom. A Coors Light beer girl cutout was tacked to the wall next to a row of rusty lockers, half of which wouldn't close. The sink thankfully had a lot of counter space around it and a large mirror behind it. The lighting was bright if not flattering, and a folding chair pulled up to the sink made do for a vanity. There was one stall with a door that didn't lock and the few female customers that came into the bar would have to scoot awkwardly around the dancers to get to it.

I popped into the stall to take a quick piss. As luck would have it I had started my period on the way over. Great. I had already agreed to work, and now I was panicked. One of the other girls on shift walked in and I poked my head over the stall door, blurting out "Hey I'm really sorry this is like my first shift ever and I just started my period and I don't know what to do about the tampon."

"Cut the string short before you put it in," she said, laughing, "I'll grab you some scissors from the bar." I rushed into the outfit I had brought: a denim mini-skirt, white camisole top, black lacy panties, and some funky sneakers with heels for my nervous legs. The other dancer came stomping back in her platforms, handing me scissors as I thanked her. "No problem. My name's Mona," she said, flashing me a big white toothed smile while she zipped back out the door. String snipped, tampon tucked, hands washed, eyeliner touched up, and I was ready to go. I took a deep breath and walked out into the bar.

I went over to the jukebox for the first time and plopped down on the vinyl stool that lived in front of it. My head spun as I took in the catalog. How in the hell was I going to strip to this shit? I decided to go with a classic rock approach. I picked "Back in Black" by AC/DC, "Girls, Girls, Girls" by Mötley Crüe, and threw in "Breaking the Law" by Judas Priest to finish things off. When the first few chords of "Back in Black" started crackling out of the speakers mounted above the stage, I trotted over and crossed paths with Mona again. She was pulling her top back on over her Double D's and gave me another encouraging smile as I climbed on stage.

The bar ran parallel to the stage and most of the customers stayed away from the rack, walking up to drop tips between mouthfuls of food. I felt like no one was watching, but every time I looked down there were a few more dollar bills at my feet. Halfway through "Girls, Girls, Girls" this guy with a long black beard and a ponytail, who towered at about six foot four, walked up and sat down. He was wearing a black Nintendo T-shirt and super baggy pants with a wallet chain. His general fashion sense made him look like a thirty-year-old roadie for the band Korn. He was the only one paying any sort of attention to me, so I danced around the stage in front of him, twirling and shaking my butt as I took off my skirt and top. When "Breaking the Law" was in full swing I got completely naked and started playing air guitar on my knees like a fucking nerd. He didn't laugh or even smile but he tipped me, and nodded as he stood when the set was over.

Breathing a sigh of relief I grabbed my pile of discarded clothes and a fistful of singles, made my way to the corner of the stage, and got dressed. The worst was over, or so I thought. I walked to the bar, fell more than sat on a stool, then worked on flattening out the single dollar bills so I could fold them into my purse. The guy next to me turned and introduced himself as Chris, offering to buy me a drink. I ordered a Jack and Coke and sucked it down, feeling relief as it calmed the butterflies in my stomach. He promptly bought me another one. We chatted about how it was my first shift, he rambled about himself and I pretended to listen, and before I knew it six songs had passed and it was my turn to plug numbers into the jukebox again.

After my second set, during which I racked up more singles and everyone continued to pay zero attention to me, I made my way back to the bathroom to check on my tampon. In the stall I pulled down my panties, squatted over the toilet, and sent an exploratory finger up. I felt nothing. Fuck. I inserted a second finger, pushed up higher and felt the bottom of the tampon but couldn't get a grip on it at all. FUCK. I hadn't just trimmed the string; I had cut the whole thing off in my zeal for hygiene. Fuck Fuck Fuck FUCK FUCK!! I stepped out of the stall and sat down for a minute to pull myself together, running hot water over my hands to warm them up. Back into the stall, this time leaning against the wall with one foot on the ground and one on top of the toilet for maximum access, I was trying to keep track of the number of songs playing outside to tell when I had to go back on stage. By my count I had three songs left.

As I rammed my fingers up my snatch, fishing for any kind of grip on the sideways tampon lodged next to my cervix, one song ended and a second one began. I kept clawing at it in a panic until I finally got a pinch of fiber, and tugged the damn thing out. It fell into the toilet with a loud PLOP and I flushed it down, spiting the handwritten "PLEASE DONT FLUSH

TAMPONS OR WIPES" sign taped up by management. I thought I had one more song left, but silence descended on the bar as the jukebox cue ended. I had counted wrong. My legs were REALLY shaking now but I managed to prep another tampon, leaving a little more string this time, ram it up there, and make a beeline to the jukebox in about 30 seconds. The bartender barked across the room at me to hurry it up and I nodded, sweating. I punched some random numbers in and sprinted to the stage in my heels like a baby deer being chased by wolves before it has fully learned how to walk.

My random number selection strategy backfired as I was serenaded by Jimmy Buffet, then Huey Lewis and the News, followed by MORE Jimmy Buffet. I managed to survive gyrating through "Cheeseburger in Paradise," and even received a few claps from the peanut gallery. When it was over I ran back to the same bar stool and collapsed. I even felt a little triumphant, like I had passed some kind of karmic stripper hazing ritual. The next few hours passed pretty uneventfully, and by the time my shift ended I had drank four Jack and Cokes, eaten a free grilled cheese, and collected about $90 in singles. I was glowing. I took a cell phone picture of myself holding the thick stack of ones in the bathroom mirror before cashing them in. I had done it. I was a real stripper. A far cry from Elizabeth Berkley in *Showgirls*, but I had successfully taken my clothes off in public and gotten paid for it. The bartender exchanged my singles for twenties and took a ten percent tip. I headed home, receiving a text on the way from the booking agent with my schedule for the rest of the week. I was ready to work 8PM-2AM Wednesday through Saturday.

So my career began. The next night I carpooled with my friend Mae, who had come with me the day before. She had a job waiting tables at a sushi joint but stripped on and off when she needed extra cash. The booking agent had hired her on the spot as well, and we spent the rest of the holiday season working there together. We lived on the opposite bank of the river from The Clubhouse, within a few blocks of each other. The freeway entrance was next to our houses, so I would pick her up each night in my 1984 Volvo with no heat, and we would drive over the bridge to drink and dance.

Wednesday night- my second shift- went a lot more smoothly. When we arrived, we were greeted at the door by the same Korn roadie who sat at my stage the day before. He turned out to be the "bouncer," hired to card people at the door and make sure customers behaved, but what he really did was watch strippers and smoke weed in the bathroom. His name was Jonathan. He would give three quick knocks before entering the ladies room, where he would pull a pipe out of a locker, hit it, and pass it to us. His deadpan reaction to my air guitar made a little more sense when I realized he was just really high all the time.

The night bartender was a tall former dancer who still had a petite figure and a sweet smile. She shook our hands and introduced herself as Bibi, immediately making us feel at home. The cook was a whole other level of weird; Corey had a bulbous nose that looked like it had been broken and reset wrong, his head covered by a tangled mop of brown hair. He had a nervous way of talking and stuttered over his words, often repeating them. "H-h-h-hi hi It's n-n-ice nice to meet you," he said, with a shit eating grin on his face, shaking my hand after being introduced by the bartender.

"Uh, Hi nice to meet you too, I'm Nikki." My dancer name was picked pretty much at random. I had spent a long time torturing over what it should be, looking up gemstones and plant names to come up with something creative. Nicotiana is the genus of the plant family containing the tobacco plant, and I thought it sounded exotic and addictive. After introducing myself as Nicotiana several times and getting "Niko ti what huh?" as a response, it took less than an hour before I was just Nikki.

Mae was much more confident that I was about her nudity and would strip buck naked every set, prancing around lip synching to whatever song she picked, like the whole world was watching and loving it. I was still easing into things but was starting to find some moves, looking less like a drunken antelope with every set. After hitting the weed pipe with Jonathan while Mae was on stage, I wandered back out into the bar lazily. It was about midnight and the place had been deserted for hours; the blue collar customers had gone home to rest up for work in the morning. The Rolling Stone's "Angie" was playing. As the song reached an emotional climax Mae bent over and grabbed her crotch from the front, pinching it in time so that her vagina seemed to say "Angie... Angie..." with Mick Jagger's voice. I collapsed in a hysterical giggling fit as the bar fell silent again. "Wait- what? Is it my turn already?" I said, gasping to catch my breath. "Uh YES GERL when my pussy is whispering ANGIE at you that means it's YOUR TURN."

At the end of the night we recapped as my car rattled back across the bridge.

"The door guy was whining about you," Mae said.

"Oh yeah? Why?"

"He came up to me and said, 'Is Nikki an amateur or something? She's hot but I went up and tipped her like ten bucks yesterday and she didn't even show me her doggy style.'"

"Uh, haha- he tipped me like four dollars and I got naked I guess, what does that even mean, *doggy style?*"

"What it sounds like dummy, get on your knees doggy style like you're getting *fucked!*"

"Shit," I said, "Show me your doggy style *bitch!*"

"Yeah, *DOGGY STYLE!!*" We laughed the whole way home.

A snowstorm descended at the end of the month, shutting down most of the city. The Clubhouse stayed open, but almost all of the dancers called and canceled. Mae and I lived so close we could still make it in. She had lived in the snow before, so she had the driving skills to glide my rust bucket of a car to work through the ten inches of snow on the ground. We picked up every shift banking on the warm building, a free meal, and free liquor to make our time worthwhile. As things turned out, we made a decent amount of cash too because it was the only place in the neighborhood that stayed open. Groups of men would come staggering in from the cold telling us they followed the bar light like the Star of Bethlehem from a mile away.

On the coldest night of the storm no customers were desperate enough to show up. Corey walked us to the car at 2:30 AM and the wind was howling. A mixture of rain and snow was coming down that chilled us all to the bone. I had been using a plastic spatula as an ice scraper for the car windshield but the ice was so thick that night we couldn't even make a dent in it.

"N-n-n-nikki, N-nikki, hey N-n-n-nikki" Corey mumbled.

"WHAT?" I spat, out of breath from smacking the ice with the handle of the spatula to no effect.

"W-we we might have s-s-something, a a scraper, I think m-m-maybe" he said.

"Ok, well go look then," Mae responded.

He disappeared for a while then came back with a metal spatula and started scraping without saying a word. As fast as he scraped a little of the ice off, the falling slush froze back onto the windshield. He kept trying for ten minutes until we finally convinced him to stop.

"C-c-cant you just start, start i-it?" He puzzled as he thought of the car's defrost as an option for the first time.

"No, the heat is broken; this car is a piece of shit."

"W-w-well, good luck!" He ran back inside without warning.

"Is he just gone now?" Mae questioned.

"Yeah.... I guess so," We looked at each other and laughed, "What a weirdo."

"Shit well, get in, I guess we can just stick our heads out the side and try not to crash"

"Oh my god."

Mae climbed into the driver's side and we folded the rear view mirrors back, since they were just as frozen over and useless as the windshield. With both the windows rolled down and scarves wrapped around our faces, we stuck our heads out and she started the car. A careful U-turn started us onto the freeway. We both got a face full of blinding snow as we drove onto the bridge and the full force of the storm hit the road. The Fremont Bridge is the biggest of the eight bridges that span the rivers. It's the one the suicides always jump from. There is a strict no pedestrian policy because of this, but desperate people still stop their cars in the middle of traffic and get out.

That night, as we rode across the Fremont Bridge the snow was thick and everything was silent. There was no other car in sight, not even any tire marks in the snow to show where others had driven. It was like we were on a ghost planet, the only ones left alive in an apocalyptic winter landscape. Mae stopped the car at the peak of the bridge.

"What are you doing?" I said.

"When are we ever going to be able to stand on this bridge again?"

"Good point," We both got out to stare over the side.

The view was breathtaking. A white blanket of snow draped the buildings downtown. Houses twinkled in the hills. The water below was black with little flecks of reflected light from the bridge cables above us. "We're sorry. We hate to interrupt," Mae began.

"But it's against the law to jump off this bridge," I joined in.

"You'll just have to kill yourself SOMEWHERE ELSE. A tourist might see you and we wouldn't want that!" We chanted Dead Kennedys into the mute night.

Suddenly another vehicle was approaching- a black Lincoln- pulling over toward us and we ran to get back into my car, squealing like kids caught skipping class.

"Are you alright?" The unknown driver pulled up beside us and shouted into the dark.

"Uh yeah we're fine we just wanted to look off the bridge!" We were relieved it wasn't a cop.

They kept driving as Mae started the car and we stuck our heads back out the windows, laughing and singing at the top of our lungs as we rolled across the rest of the bridge and down the freeway exit ramp.

SOUP IS GOOD FOOD! (We don't need you anymore)
YOU MADE A GOOD MEAL! (We don't need you anymore)
SO HOW DO YOU FEEL (We don't need you anymore)
TO BE SHIT OUT OUR ASS, AND THROWN IN THE COLD
LIKE A PIECE OF TRASH!

Years later I was working in crowded high-end clubs in Las Vegas and Los Angeles, where I would stack hundred dollar bills and ride an adrenaline high till dawn, only to crash the following night when I made next to nothing. I would look at other girls who made more money than me with their breast implants and perfect slim, tan bodies, and get frustrated to the point of tears. On those nights I found myself pausing to reflect on the frozen morning that I gleefully rode through the cold with a friend by my side, a few singles in my pocket, and a sandwich in my stomach. I would remember how that was enough.

Made in the USA
Lexington, KY
14 September 2018